Defending IoT Infrastructures with the Raspberry Pi

Monitoring and Detecting Nefarious Behavior in Real Time

Chet Hosmer

Apress®

Defending IoT Infrastructures with the Raspberry Pi: Monitoring and Detecting Nefarious Behavior in Real Time

Chet Hosmer
Longs, South Carolina, USA

ISBN-13 (pbk): 978-1-4842-3699-4   ISBN-13 (electronic): 978-1-4842-3700-7
https://doi.org/10.1007/978-1-4842-3700-7

Library of Congress Control Number: 2018949207

Managing Director, Apress Media LLC: Welmoed Spahr
Acquisitions Editor: Susan McDermott
Development Editor: Laura Berendson
Coordinating Editor: Rita Fernando

Cover designed by eStudioCalamar

Cover image designed by Freepik (www.freepik.com)

Distributed to the book trade worldwide by Springer Science+Business Media New York, 233 Spring Street, 6th Floor, New York, NY 10013. Phone 1-800-SPRINGER, fax (201) 348-4505, e-mail orders-ny@springer-sbm.com, or visit www.springeronline.com. Apress Media, LLC is a California LLC and the sole member (owner) is Springer Science + Business Media Finance Inc (SSBM Finance Inc). SSBM Finance Inc is a **Delaware** corporation.

For information on translations, please e-mail rights@apress.com, or visit http://www.apress.com/rights-permissions.

Apress titles may be purchased in bulk for academic, corporate, or promotional use. eBook versions and licenses are also available for most titles. For more information, reference our Print and eBook Bulk Sales web page at http://www.apress.com/bulk-sales.

Any source code or other supplementary material referenced by the author in this book is available to readers on GitHub via the book's product page, located at www.apress.com/9781484236994. For more detailed information, please visit http://www.apress.com/source-code.

Printed on acid-free paper

To my wife Janet; your love and guidance make the journey complete.

Table of Contents

vii

About the Author

 **Chet Hosmer** is the Founder of Python Forensics, Inc., a nonprofit organization focused on the collaborative development of open source investigative technologies using the Python programming language. Chet has been researching and developing technology and training surrounding forensics, digital investigation, and steganography for over two decades. He has made numerous appearances to discuss emerging cyberthreats, including National Public Radio's *Kojo Nnamdi Show*, ABC's *Primetime Thursday*, NHK Japan, TechTV's CyberCrime and ABC News Australia. He has also been a frequent contributor to technical and news stories relating to cybersecurity and forensics and has been interviewed and quoted by IEEE, *The New York Times*, *The Washington Post*, *Government Computer News*, Salon.com, and *Wired Magazine*.

Chet has authored five books within the cybersecurity domain, ranging from data hiding to forensics.

Chet serves as a visiting professor at Utica College in the Cybersecurity Graduate Program. He is also an adjunct faculty member at Champlain College in the Digital Forensic Science Program Masters Program.

Chet delivers keynote and plenary talks on various cybersecurity-related topics around the world each year.

About the Technical Reviewer

Michael T. Raggo
Chief Security Officer, 802 Secure (CISSP, NSA-IAM, ACE, CSI) has over 20 years of security research experience. His current focus is wireless IoT threats impacting the enterprise. Michael is the author of *Mobile Data Loss: Threats and Countermeasures* and *Data Hiding: Exposing Concealed Data in Multimedia, Operating Systems, Mobile Devices and Network Protocols* for Syngress Books, and contributing author for *Information Security: The Complete Reference* (2nd edition). A former security trainer, Michael has briefed international defense agencies including the FBI and Pentagon, is a participating member of FSISAC/BITS and PCI, and is a frequent presenter at security conferences, including Black Hat, DEF CON, Gartner, RSA, DoD Cyber Crime, OWASP, HackCon, and SANS.

Acknowledgments

A special thanks to Mike Raggo for his insight and encouragement throughout this process. Thank you for championing this project from the beginning and testing every version of the Pi sensor along the way. Your guidance, your friendship, and your quest to improve security and safety are inspiring.

Thanks to Carlton Jeffcoat and Cameron Covington at WetStone for deploying the sensor in live environments to passively map potential vulnerabilities and for providing insights to make the sensor even better.

Thanks to the Utica College cybersecurity graduate students who have experimented with the earliest to the final versions of PiSensor and have provided excellent feedback.

Thanks to Rita Fernando, Laura Berendson, Susan McDermott, and the whole team at Apress for your incredible patience throughout this process and for your constant encouragement.

Introduction

The Internet of Things (IoT) and industrial control systems (ICS) require special attention from a cybersecurity point of view. This is based on the well-known and -documented fact that the protocols and implementations have vulnerabilities that when exploited can produce considerable damage and provide an avenue for the exfiltration of data.

In addition, when examining these environments due to the dynamic nature and/or critical infrastructure implications, active scanning or probing of these environments is either discouraged or ineffective. Thus, passive monitoring of these environments offers insights into the behavior of these devices and the networks in which they operate. One of the core issues is the placement of the monitoring devices to provide visibility and coverage from both the wired and wireless points of view. There are vendor solutions that are offered today that rely on expensive hardware and software solutions that may lack flexibility.

Using a Raspberry Pi and open source Python software to passively monitor, detect, baseline, and provide insight into these behaviors has been called "crazy" by some. However, as you will see, the Raspberry Pi itself, with its multicore processor and integrated wired and wireless network components, provides the basic underpinnings necessary for a lightweight IoT/ICS sensor for less than $50.00. Couple that with an open source extensible Python software solution that dynamically reduces and records the most pertinent observations, and you have a low-cost, flexible, and nimble PiSensor for IoT and ICS environments.

CHAPTER 1

IoT Vulnerabilities

The Internet of Things (IoT) is a network of processing devices with unique identities that can connect to and transfer data over a network without requiring direct human interaction (see Figure 1-1). In many cases this makes the devices themselves autonomous or semiautonomous. They can be controlled, managed, and programmed to follow specific rules of engagement.

Interconnected autonomous devices

Limited or No Human Intervention

Supporting a variety of applications and platforms

Figure 1-1. *IoT interconnected*

The breadth of devices that currently exist as of this writing include the following:

- Health and Fitness Monitoring

- Manufacturing Systems

- Energy Metering

© Chet Hosmer 2018
C. Hosmer, *Defending IoT Infrastructures with the Raspberry Pi*,
https://doi.org/10.1007/978-1-4842-3700-7_1

- Hospital and Patient Care

- Smart Appliances and Lighting

- Enhanced Surveillance Systems

- Entertainment

- Home Automation and Security

- Multifunction Wearable Technologies

- Automotive

- Tracking Systems

- Personal Communications

- Along with new categories emerging every day

Note   The focus of this book and the accompanying source code is to observe, learn, model, and detect aberrant behavior of IoT devices using the Raspberry Pi as a sensor.

Why Is IoT Vulnerable?

When considering vulnerabilities of IoT devices and networks, we must first define the overall attack surface. If you believe Gartner's prediction (Gartner Research, 2017) that 25.1 billion IoT endpoints will exist by the year 2021[1], then this would certainly define a large attack surface. Many of these devices are also interconnected and operating across boundaries of consumers, business, industry, and government, without geographic restrictions.

---

[1]Gartner: *Forecast: Internet of Things – Endpoints and Associated Services, Worldwide 2017.* www.gartner.com/doc/3840665/ forecast-internet-things--endpoints.

Deployment options for IoT differ widely depending upon their application, industry, and defined use. However, we can generally classify IoT deployments in one of three ways: device to device, device to cloud, or device to gateway, as shown in Figures 1-2, 1-3, and 1-4.

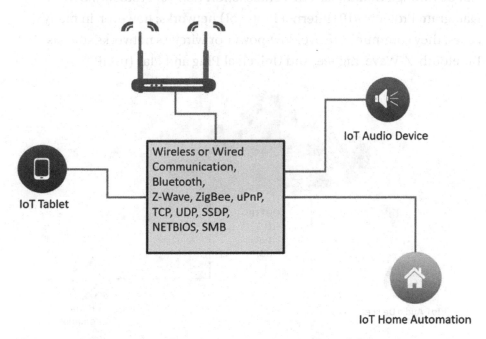

Figure 1-2. Device-to-device communication model

Device-to-Device Communication

This simple model depicts devices that directly discover, connect, and communicate using the locally available networks. The communication can be through traditional TCP (Transaction Control Protocol)/UDP (User Datagram Protocol)/IP (Internet Protocol) networks; however, in many cases, they communicate over low-power or wireless networks such as Bluetooth, Z-Wave, ZigBee, and Universal Plug and Play (uPnP).

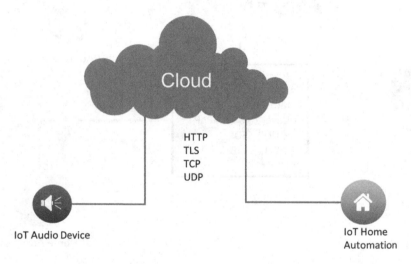

Figure 1-3. *Device-to-cloud communication*

Device-to-Cloud Communications

IoT devices using this method connect directly to an Internet-based cloud service to exchange data and control messages. This method typically utilizes traditional protocols such as TCP, UDP, HTTP(S), and TLS (Transport Layer Security) for security-based exchanges.

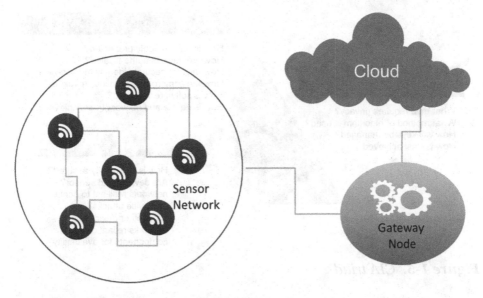

Figure 1-4. *Device-to-gateway framework*

Device-to-Gateway Sensor Network Communications

Utilizing this method, sensors discover and communicate with other sensors and coordinate information through gateways. The gateway, in turn, communicates information with other sensor networks and typically with the cloud.

At first glance, these connection and communications models don't look that different from more traditional distributed computing environments. However, many of the underlying protocols and methods of deployment are dissimilar from traditional environments and require closer examination. From a cybersecurity point of view, we still must consider and examine these environments using proven principles. At the heart, of course, is the CIA triad as shown in Figure 1-5.

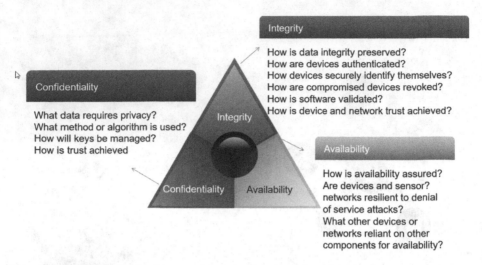

Figure 1-5. *CIA triad*

The IoT Security Foundation published the *IoT Security Compliance Framework* in 2016 to help promote contemporary best practices in IoT security. As part of the framework, they applied the CIA triad to different classes of IoT devices as shown in Figure 1-6. They defined five specific classes of IoT devices along with the security requirements of each.

- **Class 0**: Compromise of data would cause little or no impact.

- **Class 1**: Compromise of data would cause limited impact.

- **Class 2**: Devices must be resilient to attack on availability that would have significant impact.

- **Class 3**: Devices must both be resilient to attack and protect sensitive data.

- **Class 4**: Devices must be resilient to attack, preserve integrity of operation, and protect sensitive data. Any resulting breach would cause serious impact and potentially cause injury.

Compliance Class	Security Objective		
	Integrity	Availability	Confidentiality
Class 0	Basic	Basic	Basic
Class 1	Medium	Medium	Basic
Class 2	Medium	High	Medium
Class 3	Medium	High	High
Class 4	High	High	High

Figure 1-6. Compliance classification security objectives

Interpreting the security objectives at each level are defined here in Table 1-1.

Table 1-1. *Interpreting the Security Levels*

Category	Level	Requirements
Integrity	Basic	IoT devices resist low-level threat sources that have very little capability
	Medium	IoT devices resist medium-level threat sources that have minimal focused capability
	High	IoT devices must resist substantial-level threat sources
Confidentiality	Basic	IoT devices processing public information
	Medium	IoT devices protect against disclosure of low-value personally identifiable information
	High	IoT devices process very sensitive information and must protect against any disclosure
Availability	Basic	IoT device lack of availability would cause only minor disruption
	Medium	IoT devices should possess some availability defenses against the most common attacks
	High	IoT devices must anticipate determined availability attacks and take significant measures to overcome them

Moving Beyond the Basics

Now that we have set the stage of what we are up against, let's take a deeper look at what is different about IoT devices and their potential security challenges. What makes IoT devices and their accompanying protocols unique?

Low-Power Sensors - These devices may have limited processing and memory capabilities that limit the amount of traditional defensive technologies that can be integrated into them. In addition, they may only be able to communicate using low-power protocols such as Bluetooth, ZigBee, or Z-Wave, thus obscuring their behavior on either the local area network (LAN) or WIFI network.

Single Board Computers and Embedded Operating Systems - To reduce cost and power requirements, many IoT devices use small inexpensive hardware platforms such as Raspberry Pi, WeMO, Arduino, Intel Edison, and Quark. These devices are capable of running embedded operating systems such as Raspbian, Snappy Ubuntu, FreeBSD, Kali Linux, and Windows 10 IoT Core along with other lesser-known open source and proprietary systems such as RTOS IoT, Nano-RK, TinyOS, Mantis, and Mbed. As you might have already guessed, some of these operating systems have NOT been thoroughly vetted for security vulnerabilities. Furthermore, since some of the most popular are open source, the ability for adversaries to identify and then exploit design and/or coding flaws is a potential threat.

Zero Configuration Devices - All configuration of these devices is done automatically (without manual intervention) simply by applying power. This generates a network ready state that typically requires three steps:

- Address allocation without the need of a DHCP (Dynamic Host Configuration Protocol) server

- Name translation without access to a predefined Domain Name Service

- Ability to discover other devices that are nearby or located on the same subnet, WIFI network, or other low-power wireless network

Dynamic Discovery Protocols - Protocols such as uPnP, Simple Service Discovery Protocol (SSDP), and Network Basic Input/Output System (NETBIOS) with Server Message Block are just a few of the examples that are commonly used. Typically, IoT devices need to discover services available to them. NETBIOS with Server Message Block allows devices to advertise services and then determine their status.

Use of Multicast Communication - Protocols such as Web Services Dynamic Discovery can identify services available on the LAN. Web Services Dynamic Discovery can communicate on top of SOAP (Simple Object Access Protocol), which in turn can run on top of HTTP, SMTP, TCP, UDP, and even the Java Message Service (JMS).

All of these communication and discovery protocols make it difficult to track behavior, control access, ensure security, and even continuously monitor these dynamic behaviors.

What Unique Vulnerabilities Lurk Within IoT Devices?

Our research shows that a plethora of vulnerabilities exists within the IoT domain. This list represents several key high-level concerns.

- Hardware platforms and embedded operating systems built for low cost and low power potentially contain a wide variety of untapped vulnerabilities versus traditional desktop and mobile devices.

- Direct discovery and connection between local IoT devices has the potential of enabling self-replicating malware threats once a single device or manufacturer has been compromised.

10

- Direct connection of IoT devices to the Internet and cloud-based services can circumvent traditional proven security mechanisms and frameworks.

- Lightweight protocols with limited built-in strong authentication, data privacy, or denial of service defenses capabilities are targets for those wishing to obtain access, leak information, or disrupt operation of target IoT devices and sensor networks.

What Are the Common IoT Attack Vectors?

Several recent successful attacks against IoT devices have helped to reveal common attack vectors. During DEF CON 23 and 24 (2015–2016) the IoT Village was launched to focus attention on the vulnerabilities found in IoT devices. The combined result produced 66 new zero day vulnerabilities from 18 different manufacturers and over 20 unique devices. The vulnerabilities included the following:

- Device Backdoors

- Lack of Encryption

- Poor Key Management and Key Protection

- Plain Text Passwords

- Buffer Overflows

- Command Injection Exploits

- SQL (Structured Query Language) Injections

In addition, other devices such as SmartTVs, home assistants, and the devices that they control are being targeted:

- SmartTV Data Leaks (Samsung and LG)

- Alexa and Google Home can be hacked to monitoring everything you watch and say. These systems control lights, fans, switches, thermostats, garage doors, sprinklers, door locks provided from numerous vendors such as: WeMo, Philips Hue, Samsung SmartThings, Nest, and ecobee

This represents just a glimpse at the attack surface related to IoT devices to give you a flavor of the threats and risks associated with IoT devices, protocols, and platforms.

How Do the Raspberry Pi and Python Fit In?

As the book title *Defending IoT Infrastructures with the Raspberry Pi* implies, we will be developing a Raspberry Pi sensor written in Python. The Pi will be used to model, monitor, analyze, and report aberrant behavior emanating from IoT devices along with targeted attacks perpetrated against those devices.

Raspberry Pi Brief Introduction

There are literally hundreds of books, videos, tutorials, and online resources that provide a thorough background on the Raspberry Pi. Thus, this quick introduction assumes that the reader have familiarity with the Raspberry Pi. However, I want to provide a focused definition of how I plan to use the Pi as an IoT sensor. It turns out that many IoT devices based on the Raspberry Pi already exist. In addition, the Windows IoT core now runs on a Raspberry Pi offering developers both Linux (Raspbian and other flavors) along with Windows as a choice for development.

Raspberry Pi Hardware

Figure 1-7 is a snapshot of the Raspberry Pi 3 Model B that we will be using for this project.

Figure 1-7. *Raspberry Pi 3 Model B*

The key features of this single board device that are important for our work that are built into the standard product include the following:

- CPU: 1.2 GHZ quad-core ARM Cortex A53 (ARMv8 Instruction Set): Leveraging each core for specific functions will be critical in capturing and identifying IoT device behaviors.

- Memory: 1 GB LPDDR2-900 SDRAM: Utilizing the expanded memory of Pi 3, will help to reduce I/O to the slower SD device.

13

- Network: 10/100 MBPS Ethernet, 802.11n Wireless
  LAN, Bluetooth 4.0: The built-in networking option
  allows for the use of core functions of the Pi for the
  main network monitoring interfaces whether they be
  wired ethernet, WIFI, or Bluetooth devices.

- USB ports: 4: Provides the needed expansion
  opportunities to support other wireless technologies
  such as ZigBee.

All of this comes in a package that costs under $40.00 for the single
board device. Adding in the cost of a fast 32-GB SD Card and a computer
kit keeps the cost under $100.

Raspbian OS

In addition to the Pi itself, we will be using the Raspbian Operating System
on the Pi. Specifically, I will be using Raspbian GNU/Linux 8 (Jessie). As we
move into later chapters I will provide details of the OS configuration and
security measures.

Python

Python is the language of choice for all the software components being
developed. We will be using Python 2.7.9, which is the latest 2.7.x version
available for the Pi as of this writing. With minor modification, the code
will run on Python 3.x as well. With a couple of exceptions, I will be
only be using the Python Standard Library modules, thus eliminating
the need to install or most importantly understand the underpinning,
performance, and risks associated with third-party libraries. This is mainly
a performance and security decision that will keep the Pi as minimal and
safe as possible. The book is not designed to teach you Python, as there
are many resources that can help you with that. However, all my Python
code is extensively documented and the rationale for the methods and

approaches chosen are detailed throughout the book to hopefully extend your knowledge.

Note   There are many outstanding third-party Python libraries and modules out there for you to experiment with as well.

Summary

This chapter provided a very brief introduction to the IoT landscape present and future. In addition, it examined some of the basic differences between IoT devices and more traditional computing devices. We examined several classes of vulnerabilities and exploits of IoT devices to get a flavor for the diversity we face today and in the future. Finally, we provide a brief introduction to the Raspberry Pi, the Raspbian operating system, and the Python programming language that will be utilized throughout this book.

In Chapter 2, we will examine possible methods to model IoT environments for passively monitoring their behavior and ultimately discover aberrant behaviors.

CHAPTER 2

Classifying and Modeling IoT Behavior

In Chapter 1 we took a high-level look at the differences between IoT environments and traditional computing environments. In addition, we examined some of the unique risks and vulnerabilities associated with IoT environments along with the unique discovery and communication protocols that are in use. These characteristics led me to focus on passive mapping and monitoring of IoT behavior. The rationale for this decision includes the following:

- Many unique devices exist.

- These devices can be temporal, meaning that they may appear and disappear from networks.

- They can operate on different wireless and wired networks.

- They can communicate directly with each other, in many cases without supervision or use of an intermediary such as a switch or wireless access point.

- New devices can be added by simply applying power to them as with zero configuration devices.

© Chet Hosmer 2018
C. Hosmer, *Defending IoT Infrastructures with the Raspberry Pi*,
https://doi.org/10.1007/978-1-4842-3700-7_2

- They can utilize one of several dynamic discover protocols.

- Finally, if devices are compromised they may impact other local devices, leak information, or disrupt activities of other devices and networks.

Thus, the remainder of this book will focus on the collection, mapping, monitoring, and ultimately the detection of rogue devices or abnormal behavior of IoT devices. To accomplish this, we must ask a few critical questions.

1. What passive observations data should we collect?

2. How should we categorize collected observations as meaningful, redundant, or plain noise?

3. How might we organize and store the observations?

4. What do we plan to do with the collected observations?

   a. How will we define "normal" versus "abnormal" behavior?

   b. Can the collected observations be used to train machine learning elements?

   c. Can the observations be a viable source of forensic evidence?

5. What networks should we passively monitor?

6. What observations will be recorded based on this passive monitoring?

7. Are we really going to use a Raspberry Pi to do this?

Clearly, we are not going to address these all of these questions at the same time. Rather, let's develop a model for the basics and then we can build upon that model in a spiral fashion.

We will do this by starting with what we already know well, Ethernet-based IP wired networks. To monitor and collect data we can use a variety of off-the-shelf tools or we can roll our own. Because we are planning to deploy this technology on a Raspberry Pi, using Python (I know, sounds crazy, right?), we need to keep this as simple and as close to the metal as possible. Thus, for this first experiment, I will be only using the Python standard socket library to perform this collection, and I will be using the built-in Python dictionary type to store, categorize, and at the same time, reduce the observations.

What Should We Collect?

Let's take a very simplistic view of a traditional wired network. Devices would be attached to a physical switch, with a SPAN or monitoring port. A packet capture device would be connected to the monitoring port and record all observed packets in and out of the switch (see Figure 2-1).

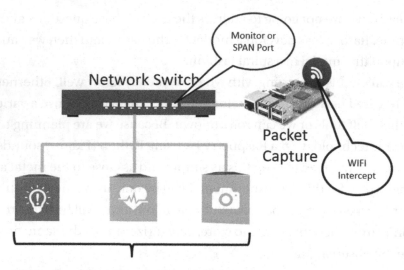

Figure 2-1. *Simplified LAN diagram*

Starting with the basics, we will examine the packets that could be monitored using this approach. To break this down, for the first example we plan to collect, record, and observe the following:

1. Ethernet Packets

2. ARP (Address Resolution Protocol) Packets

3. IP Packets

4. TCP Packets

5. UDP Packets

6. ICMP (Internet Control Message Protocol) Packets

Ethernet Packet Format

Examining the Ethernet header (see Figure 2-2), we narrow in on the destination and source media access control address, (commonly referred to as MAC address), along with the type/length field. These provide important mapping information, protocol data, and also the ability to look up the manufacturer associated with the source and destination of the packet.

Sample Ethernet Packet

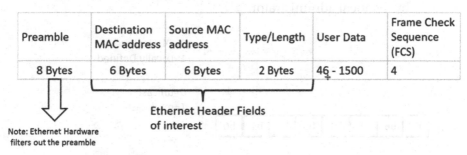

Preamble	Destination MAC address	Source MAC address	Type/Length	User Data	Frame Check Sequence (FCS)
8 Bytes	6 Bytes	6 Bytes	2 Bytes	46 - 1500	4

Note: Ethernet Hardware filters out the preamble

Ethernet Header Fields of interest

Figure 2-2. Ethernet packet overview

Note   Network device MAC addresses can be modified in many cases. Thus, it is possible to modify such devices to report an inaccurate or spoofed organizationally unique identifier (OUI).

Breaking down the first octet (byte), we see that bit 0 and bit 1 have special meaning (see Figure 2-3).

1. Bit 0 defines whether the packet is set to all nodes individually (**unicast**) or if only one packet is sent (**multicast**) and individual NICs can decide to accept or reject the packet.

2. Bit 1 defines whether the MAC address is defined **globally** through **OUI registration** or whether the MAC address set by the manufacturer is **overridden** by the local administrator.

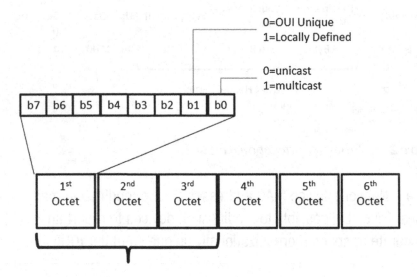

Organizationally Unique Identifier (OUI)

Figure 2-3. *OUI breakdown*

Our objective in extracting the MAC address is to map the packet to a specific device. If the MAC address is not locally defined, then extract information about the device defined by the manufacturer.

ARP

The ARP is used to dynamically discover the mapping of devices operating on a network. This maps the MAC address (layer 2) with the IP address (layer 3).

For example, Device A needs to communicate with Device B, but requires the MAC address to do so as Device A's ARP table is incomplete (see Figure 2-4). Device B responds to the request allowing device A to map the layer 2 MAC address with the layer 3 IP address to allow Device A to properly address Device B at the Ethernet and IP layers.

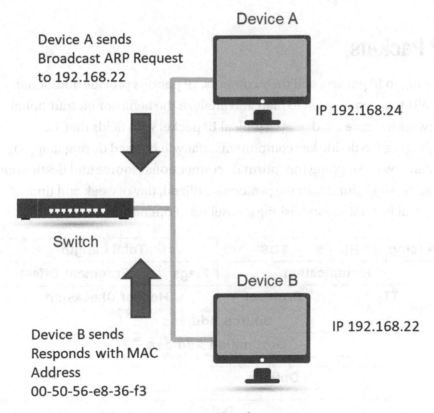

Figure 2-4. *Simplified ARP request/replay process*

Mapping ARP behavior (request, replies, frequency, and time frame) can identify devices that are behaving normally, or devices that could be rogue, are new to the network, or are operating erratically or maliciously. Mapping such behaviors under "normal conditions" will help to identify aberrant conditions.

ARP Tables   In Ethernet, LAN, a table, also referred to as the ARP cache, is used to maintain a correlation between each MAC address and its corresponding IP address.

IP Packets

Moving to IP packets and their contents, IP packets provide additional details that can be used to map and analyze the behavior on traditional networks. Figure 2-5 depicts a typical IP packet with fields that are highlighted to define key components that will be used during mapping and analysis. Mapping the "normal" connections (source and destination IP addresses) along with the protocols utilized, day of week and time of day, will be vital in establishing a baseline of operations.

Version	IP HL	TOS	Total Length	
Identification			Flags	Fragment Offset
TTL		Protocol	Header Checksum	
Source Address				
Destination Address				
Options			Pad	
Data				

Figure 2-5. *IP packets*

Next, we will examine the specific data contained in the associated data (for example TCP, UDP, and ICMP) contents delivered using IP packets.

TCP Packets

Extracting specific source and destination ports from TCP packets, as shown in Figure 2-6, again provides a model for determining "normal" behavior on the network. TCP packets provide reliable link capabilities by using sequence and acknowledgement numbers to ensure orderly delivery and acknowledgment of packets. If packets are lost or delayed, the protocol will retry and request retransmission. At this point we will be ignoring the payload of the packet and just focus on the source and destination ports, as they contain the most meaningful information that can be reasonably and quickly acquired. Port values range from 1 to 65535 and are generally defined here:

1. Ports 1–1023 are considered well-known ports.

2. Ports 1024–49151 are considered "registered ports" that are assigned by the Internet Assigned Numbers Authority (IANA).

3. Ports 49152–65535 are considered dynamic, private, or more commonly ephemeral (i.e., lasting for a brief time or transient). For example, ports in this range are commonly used by clients making a connection to a server. It should be noted that some of the ports in this range have been mapped to known malware usage.

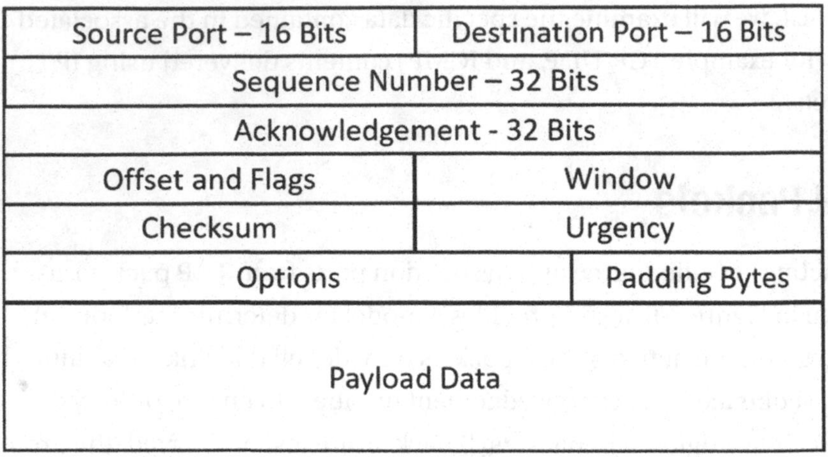

Source Port – 16 Bits	Destination Port – 16 Bits
Sequence Number – 32 Bits	
Acknowledgement - 32 Bits	
Offset and Flags	Window
Checksum	Urgency
Options	Padding Bytes
Payload Data	

Figure 2-6. *TCP packet details*

UDP Packet

UDP packets, unlike TCP packets, ensure orderly packet sequencing. UDP packets are connectionless and less reliable (see Figure 2-7). The protocol is used for streaming data where packets that are lost or are out of sequence will not impact the communication. Again, we are interested here in mapping the normal behavior by capturing the source and destination port numbers as discussed in the TCP section.

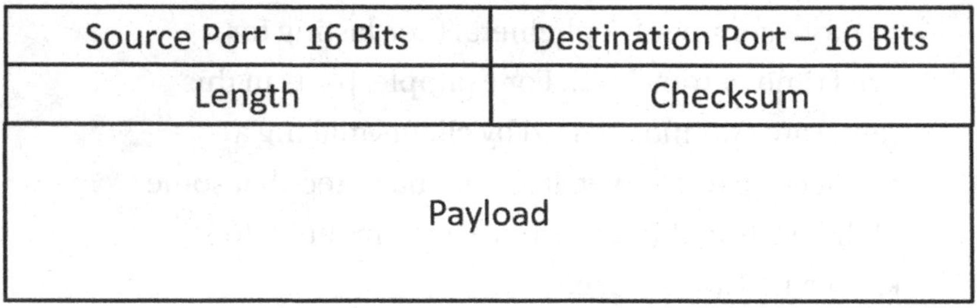

Source Port – 16 Bits	Destination Port – 16 Bits
Length	Checksum
Payload	

Figure 2-7. *UDP packet details*

ICMP Packet

ICMP defines a protocol that provides troubleshooting, control, and error message services. ICMP is most frequently used to diagnose and test connections on an IP network. The only information we will be concerned with is the fact that an ICMP packet was sent over the network from a source IP address to a destination IP address (see Figure 2-8). Note that there is not a port number associated with ICMP.

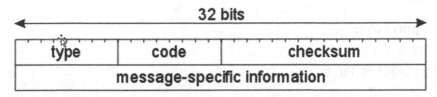

Figure 2-8. ICMP packet details

Passively Monitoring IoT Behavior

Compared to active probing, passive monitoring provides greater insight into the activities of the network being monitored. The difference can be likened to a movie versus a still photograph. Using tools like NMAP to identify devices operating on your network provides an instantaneous view of those devices that properly respond. In many cases IoT devices are transient and thus could and will be missed by active or probing-based methods. Mapping the behavior of these devices over an extended period of time is critical to understanding the potential threats that they pose, along with connections to other devices.

Modeling Normal Behavior

Now that we have defined several key elements from the Ethernet layer, IP layer, and transport layers, let's take inventory of the key elements that we could observe and determine how we can store and categorize these observed values.

Ethernet Layer

```
Source MAC address
Destination MAC address
Frame Type (IPv4, IPv6, ARP)
```

IP Layer

```
Source IP
Destination IP
Protocol
```

Transport Layer

```
Source Port
Destination Port
```

Because it is likely that we will encounter many packets with the same MAC, source IP, destination IP, protocol, and nonephemeral port values, we need to reduce the data that we store regarding these observations. We will also be choosing a data type that is built in. We could choose a Python list or set, but both have limitations that make them not the best choice. However, the built-in dictionary data type in Python provides the ideal solution for storing these observations.

Python dictionaries, much like traditional Webster-style dictionaries, have a key and a value, which is typically referred to as a key/value pair. In Python both the key and the value can be complex, the only rule being that the key must be a hashable type such as an integer, long, string, or tuple. The value part of the key/value pair can be a list or other nonhashable data type.

The question is how would we structure the key to help us reduce the observations that we need to store and begin to build and hold a model of normal behavior. To simplify the question: what combination of fields from the collected observations would be considered unique?

I'm going to use the following tuple as the key:

(SRC-MAC, DST-MAC, SRC-IP, DST-IP, Protocol, Port)

Notice I didn't include SRC and DST port. The reason is that when a client makes a connection to a server, the port that is chosen is dynamic and normally comes from the ephemeral set of ports. Thus, the port that will be included in the key will be the nonephemeral port. If both ports are nonephemeral then two entries will be made in the dictionary, one using the SRC port and one using the DST port. If both ports are ephemeral, again both entries will be made.

So that takes care of the key. Now the question is what does the value portion of the key/value pair contain?

For this we are interested in keeping track of the number of occurrences of each unique combination. Furthermore, we would like to keep track of when and how often that combination occurred. Therefore, I will use a list to keep track of the number of occurrences of each unique key. Note, keeping track of the number of occurrences can be very fine-grained (down to the hour, day, day of week, etc.). To keep this simple, and use this data later for machine learning, I have decided to break the occurrences count down in the following way.

Early Morning: 12:00 AM-5:59 AM

Morning: 6:00 AM-11:59 AM

Afternoon: 12:00 PM-5:59 PM

Evening: 6:00 PM-11:59 PM

Weekend: 12:00 AM Saturday-11:59 PM Sunday

Therefore, the value list will be initialized with just five occurrence count values:

[0,0,0,0,0]

Each time a new observation is made with the **same key**, the number associated with that time will be incremented by one in the value argument associated with that key.

How Can This Be Accomplished on a Raspberry Pi with Python?

I promise to only say this once: It's as easy as Pie.

Part I: Passively Capture Packets in Python on a Raspberry Pi

1. As depicted in Figure 2-1 we need to attach the Pi to a monitoring or SPAN port of an Ethernet switch along with the WIFI 802.11 air waves.

2. Next, we need to place the Pi Ethernet Port into promiscuous mode.

3. Finally, we need to capture packets using the Python standard socket library.

Examine a Simple Code Snippet to Perform These Operations

The code snippet written in Python performs three basic operations (see Listing 2-1).

1. The code places the standard Ethernet port of the Pi into promiscuous mode. This allows us to view any traffic flowing over the network even if it is not destined or originating from the Pi itself.

2. The code opens a socket associated with the Ethernet port to listen to traffic passing over the network.

3. The code captures a single packet and displays the results in hexadecimal.

Listing 2-1. sniff.py Capture One Packet with Python

```
'''

Capture a single packet in promiscuous mode
Note: you must run this script as super user
i.e. sudo python sniff.py
'''

import os                # Python operating system standard library
import socket            # Python low level socket standard library
import sys               # Python system standard library
from binascii import hexlify  # Python binary ascii conversions
                                              standard library

# configure Raspberry Pi eth0 in promiscuous mode
# using a system command
try:
    ret =  os.system("ifconfig eth0 promisc")
except Exception as err:
    print "System Command Failed: ", str(err)
    sys.exit(0)

if ret == 0:
    # If the command was successful
    print 'Promiscuous Mode Set Correctly'

    # create a new socket using the python socket module
    # PF_PACKET    : Specifies Protocol Family Packet Level
```

```
# SOCK_RAW        : Specifies A raw protocol at the network
                    layer
# htons(0x0800) : Specifies all headers and packets
#                 : Ethernet and IP, including TCP/UDP etc

try:
        # attempt to open the socket for capturing raw packets
        rawSocket=socket.socket(socket.PF_PACKET,socket.
        SOCK_RAW,
            socket.htons(0x0800))
except Exception as err:
    # catch any exceptions and report the error
    print "Socket Error", str(err)
    sys.exit(0)

# If socket is established and we have established
promiscuous mode
print "Network       : Promiscuous Mode"
print "Sniffer       : Ready: \n"

# attempt to receive a packet
# Note: this function call is synchronous, thus it will wait)
try:
    recvPacket=rawSocket.recv(65535)
    print "Packet Received:"
    print hexlify(recvPacket)
    print "\nEnd"
except Exception as err:
    # Catch any exceptions and report the error
    print "Receive Socket Error: ", str(err)
    sys.exit(0)
else:
    print "System Command Failed to set promiscuous mode"
```

Sample Execution of the Script

When executing this script we need to have privilege. In other words, we need to be operating as superuser (sudo) in order to place the network interface card (NIC) into promiscuous mode. Next, since the script is written in Python we need to invoke the Python interpreter (python). Finally, we need to identify the script (sniff.py) we are executing. The script then performs as expected, setting the NIC into promiscuous mode, capturing a single packet and displaying the packet details in hex (see Listing 2-2).

Listing 2-2. Sample Hex Dump of a Received Packet

```
pi@raspberrypi:~/Desktop $ sudo python sniff.py
Promiscuous Mode Set Correctly
Network      : Promiscuous Mode
Sniffer      : Ready:

Packet Received:
0000ca11223314b31f07219e080045000282731400080064d8bc0a8006da2
7d2281e70c01bba0c0a5de4e0b8d0b501101001e420000000000000000

End
```

Part II: Identify and Extract the Key Packet Components

The next step in the process is to capture and then parse the packet contents. This includes extracting the Ethernet, IP, ARP, TCP, ICMP, IGMP, and UDP components in our first example.

You may notice a new entry in the list IGMP. The IGMP protocol is used to establish multicast group memberships. Multicast protocols are commonly used by IoT devices in order to discover nearby devices along with the services that they offer.

To handle this, I have created a new Python script called "PacketRecorder.py" which continually captures packets, extracts the key information, and records the occurrences of each unique combination in a Python dictionary.

Let's take a deeper look at some of the key components of the script (see Listing 2-3). At the end of the chapter I will provide the complete source code for the script.

Listing 2-3. PacketRecorder.py Script Overview

```
Overview and Copyright

'''

PacketRecorder.py
version .50
July 2017
Author: C. Hosmer, Python Forensics

Requirements:
Python 2.7.9 or greater
Raspbian or Ubuntu Linux

Copyright (c) 2017 Python Forensics and Chet Hosmer

Permission is hereby granted, free of charge, to any person
obtaining a copy of this software and associated documentation
files (the "Software"), to deal in the Software without
restriction,including without limitation the rights to use, copy,
modify, merge, publish, distribute, sublicense, and/or sell copies
of the Software, and to permit persons to whom the Software is
furnished to do so, subject to the following conditions:

The above copyright notice and this permission notice shall be
included in all copies or substantial portions of the Software.

'''
```

34

Required Python Standard and Third-Party Libraries

For this script, I will be using almost exclusively standard Python libraries to perform the operations. I have imported one third-party library, *PrettyTable*, to provide tabular results of the recording (see Listing 2-4).

Listing 2-4. Required Libraries

```
''' Import Python Standard Library Modules '''
import datetime
import calendar
import pickle
import struct
import os
import socket
import sys
import signal
from binascii import hexlify

# 3rd Party Libraries
from prettytable import PrettyTable
```

The Script Main Loop

Taking a top-down look at the script, let's first examine the main script entry point in Listing 2-5. Note that this script is completely contained in a single file (not including the importing of the standard and third-party libraries).

The script performs the following operations:

1. Creates a PacketProcessor object that will be used to extract and record key information from each packet.

2. Configures Ethernet port 0 on the Raspberry Pi in promiscuous mode.

35

3.   Creates a raw socket using this promiscuous port.

4.   Sets a signal timer to capture packets for 1 hour
     (3600 seconds).

5.   Creates a loop to receive packets.

6.   Each received packet is then passed to the
     PacketExtractor method of the PacketProcessing
     object.

7.   Finally, once the timer expires the PrintMap method
     of the PacketProcessing object is called to print out
     the results.

Listing 2-5. PacketRecorder Main Loop

```
# Main Script Starts Here
#====================================

if __name__ == '__main__':

    "Python Packet Recorder v.50"
    "Python Forensics, Inc.  July 2017 \n"

    # create a packet processing object
    packetObj = PacketProcessor()

    # Python Packet Capture
    # configure the eth0 in promiscuous mode
    try:
        ret =  os.system("ifconfig eth0 promisc")
    except Exception as err:
        print "System Command Failed: ", str(err)
        sys.exit(0)
```

```python
if ret == 0:
    print 'Promiscuous Mode Enabled for eth0'

    # create a new socket using the python socket module
    # PF_PACKET    : Specifies Protocol Family Packet Level
    # SOCK_RAW     : Specifies A raw protocol at the
    #                  network layer
    # htons(0x0800) : Specifies all headers and packets
    #                : Ethernet and IP, including TCP/UDP etc

    # attempt to open the socket for capturing raw packets

    try:
        rawSocket=socket.socket(socket.PF_PACKET,socket.
        SOCK_RAW,
                    socket.htons(0x0800))
    except Exception as err:
        print "Socket Error", str(err)
        sys.exit(0)

    print "Packet Processor        : Ready: \n"

    # Set signal to 1 hour
    signal.signal(signal.SIGALRM, handler)
    signal.alarm(3600)

    try:
        while True:
            # attempt to receive (synchronous call)
            try:
                recvPacket=rawSocket.recv(65535)
                packetObj.PacketExtractor(recvPacket)
            except Exception as err:
                packetObj.printMap()
```

```
                    print "Receive Socket Error: ", str(err)
                    sys.exit(0)
        except myTimeout:
            packetObj.printMap()
            packetObj.SaveOb("observations.pickle")
            print "\nEnd Packet Processor"
            sys.exit(0)
    else:
        print "System Command Failed to set promiscuous mode"
```

PacketProcessor Class

The PacketProcessor class contains four basic methods (see Listing 2-6):

1. __Init__ or the constructor: This function is called
    when an object is instantiated from the class. It
    creates two lookup objects for converting Ethernet
    frame types and transport protocol numbers to
    readable values. It also creates an empty dictionary
    to hold the key/value pairs observed.

2. PacketExtractor: This function processes the
    observed packet data. It extracts key information
    from the Ethernet frame, IP header, and transport
    protocols. Once the required information is
    collected, the key will be equal to SRC-MAC,
    DST-MAC, SRC-IP, DST-IP, protocol, and port, and
    the value will be equal to the observed occurrence
    times. A dictionary entry is created or updated
    based on the observed data from the packet.

3. PrintMap: This function iterates through each of the
    entries in the dictionary of recorded observations
    and prints them in a table format (see Figure 2-9).

4. SaveObservations: This function uses the Python
    pickle library to save the dictionary as a pickle file.
    We will be recalling this dictionary in later chapters
    to perform additional operations and analysis
    and to use as a key input to the machine learning
    process.

Listing 2-6. PacketProcessor Class

```
class PacketProcessor:
    """

    Packet Processor Class Methods
    __init__ Constructor
    PacketProcessor(self, packet) : processes a single packet
    PrintMap(self) : prints out the content of the map
    """
    def __init__(self):
        """"Constructor"""
        '''

        Create Lookup Objects

        These Object provide lookups for:
        Ethernet Frame Types
        Transport Protocol Types
        '''

        self.traOBJ  = TRANSPORT()
        self.ethOBJ  = ETH()

        # Packet Dictionary
        self.d = {}
```

```python
def PacketExtractor(self, packet):
    ''' Extract Packet Data input: string packet, dictionary d
        result is to update dictionary d
    '''

    ETH_LEN  = 14      # ETHERNET HDR LENGTH
    IP_LEN   = 20      # IP HEADER    LENGTH
    UDP_LEN  = 8       # UDP HEADER   LENGTH

    ''' Elements of the key '''

    self.srcMac = ''
    self.dstMac = ''
    self.srcIP  = ''
    self.dstIP  = ''
    self.proto  = ''
    self.port   = ''

    EthernetHeader=packet[0:ETH_LEN]
    ethFields =struct.unpack("!6s6sH",EthernetHeader)

    self.dstMac = hexlify(ethFields[0])
    self.srcMac = hexlify(ethFields[1])
    self.fType  = ethFields[2]

    frameType = self.ethOBJ.lookup(self.fType)

    if frameType == "IPv4":
        # Process as IPv4 Packet
        ipHeader = packet[ETH_LEN:ETH_LEN+IP_LEN]

        # unpack the ip header fields
        ipHeaderTuple = struct.unpack('!BBHHHBBH4s4s' ,
        ipHeader)
```

```
# extract the key ip header fields of interest
                                         # Field
                                           Contents
verLen       = ipHeaderTuple[0]          # Field 0:
                                           Ver and
                                           Length
protocol     = ipHeaderTuple[6]          # Field 6:
                                           Protocol
                                           Number
sourceIP     = ipHeaderTuple[8]          # Field 8:
                                           Source IP
destIP       = ipHeaderTuple[9]          # Field 9:
                                           Destination
                                           IP

# Calculate / Convert extracted values

version      = verLen >> 4       # Upper Nibble is
                                   the version Number
length       = verLen & 0x0F     # Lower Nibble
                                   represents the size
ipHdrLength  = length * 4        # Calculate the
                                   header in bytes

# convert the src/dst IP address to typical dotted
notation strings

self.srcIP = socket.inet_ntoa(sourceIP);
self.dstIP = socket.inet_ntoa(destIP);

translate = self.traOBJ.lookup(str(protocol))
transProtocol = translate[0]

if transProtocol == 'TCP':
```

```python
        self.proto = "TCP"

        stripTCPHeader =
                packet[ETH_LEN+ipHdrLength:ipHdr
                Length+ETH_LEN+IP_LEN]

        # unpack the TCP Header to obtain the
        # source and destination port

        tcpHeaderBuffer = struct.unpack('!HHLLBBHHH',
        stripTCPHeader)

        self.srcPort = tcpHeaderBuffer[0]
        self.dstPort = tcpHeaderBuffer[1]

    elif transProtocol == 'UDP':

        self.proto = "UDP"

        stripUDPHeader =
            packet[ETH_LEN+ipHdrLength:ETH_
            LEN+ipHdrLength+UDP_LEN]

        # unpack the UDP packet and obtain the
        # source and destination port

        udpHeaderBuffer = struct.unpack('!HHHH',
        stripUDPHeader)

        self.srcPort = udpHeaderBuffer[0]
        self.dstPort = udpHeaderBuffer[1]

    elif transProtocol == 'ICMP':

        self.proto = "ICMP"
        self.srcPort = ""
```

```
        self.dstPort = ""
    elif transProtocol == 'IGMP':

        self.proto = "IGMP"
        self.srcPort = ""
        self.dstPort = ""
    else:
        self.proto = transProtocol
        self.srcPort = ""
        self.dstPort = ""

elif frameType == 'ARP':
    self.proto = "ARP"
    self.srcPort = ""
    self.dstPort = ""

else:
    self.proto = frameType
    self.srcPort = ""
    self.dstPort = ""

valueNdx = getOccurrenceValue()

# get the most unique port to use
portA, portB = getUniquePort(self.srcPort, self.
dstPort)

# create the key for this packet
key = (self.srcMac, self.dstMac, self.srcIP, self.
dstIP,
       self.proto, portA)

try:
    value = self.d[key]
```

```
            # Increment the appropriate occurrence value
            value[valueNdx] = value[valueNdx] + 1
            self.d[key] = value
        except:
            # New Key initialize the value
            value = [0,0,0,0,0]
            value[valueNdx] = value[valueNdx] + 1
            self.d[key] = value

        if portB != None:
            # create a 2nd key for this packet
            key = (self.srcMac, self.dstMac, self.srcIP,
                    self.dstIP, self.proto, portB)

        try:
            value = seld.d[key]
            # Increment the appropriate occurrence value
            value[valueNdx] = value[valueNdx] + 1
            self.d[key] = value
        except:
            # New Key initialize the value
            value = [0,0,0,0,0]
            value[valueNdx] = value[valueNdx] + 1
            self.d[key] = value

    def printMap(self):
        ''' Print the contents of the packet map'''

        ''' Table Heading'''
        t = PrettyTable(['srcMac', 'DstMac', 'SrcIP', 'DstIP',
        'Protocol',
                        'Port', '-->', "12AM>", "06AM>",
                        "12PM>", "06PM>", "SAT-SUN"])
```

```
        for eachKey in self.d:
            value = self.d[eachKey]
            t.add_row([eachKey[0], eachKey[1], eachKey[2],
            eachKey[3],
                        eachKey[4], eachKey[5]," ", str(value[0]),
                        str(value[1]), str(value[2]), str(value[3]),
                        str(value[4])])

        t.align = "l"
        print t.get_string(sortby="SrcIP")

    def SaveOb(self, fileName):
        ''' Save the current observation dictionary to a file '''
        with open(fileName, 'wb') as fp:
            pickle.dump(self.d, fp)
```

```
pi@raspberrypi:~/Desktop $ sudo python packetrecorder.py
Python Packet Recorder v.50
Python Forensics, Inc.  July 2017
```

```
| srcMac      | DstMac       | SrcIP           | DstIP           | Protocol | Port | --> | 12AM> | 06AM> | 12PM> | 06PM> | SAT-SUN |
+-------------+--------------+-----------------+-----------------+----------+------+-----+-------+-------+-------+-------+---------+
| 10ae60825b58| ffffffffffff | 0.0.0.0         | 255.255.255.255 | UDP      | 67   |     | 0     | 0     | 0     | 1     | 0       |
| 10ae60825b58| ffffffffffff | 0.0.0.0         | 255.255.255.255 | UDP      | 68   |     | 0     | 0     | 0     | 1     | 0       |
| 40b4cdb12685| ffffffffffff | 0.0.0.0         | 255.255.255.255 | UDP      | 67   |     | 1     | 0     | 0     | 0     | 0       |
| 40b4cdb12685| ffffffffffff | 0.0.0.0         | 255.255.255.255 | UDP      | 68   |     | 1     | 0     | 0     | 0     | 0       |
| 74754880f3a2| ffffffffffff | 0.0.0.0         | 255.255.255.255 | UDP      | 67   |     | 0     | 0     | 0     | 1     | 0       |
| 74754880f3a2| ffffffffffff | 0.0.0.0         | 255.255.255.255 | UDP      | 68   |     | 0     | 0     | 0     | 1     | 0       |
| 789f70a4c254| ffffffffffff | 0.0.0.0         | 255.255.255.255 | UDP      | 67   |     | 1     | 0     | 0     | 0     | 0       |
| 789f70a4c254| ffffffffffff | 0.0.0.0         | 255.255.255.255 | UDP      | 68   |     | 1     | 0     | 0     | 3     | 0       |
| cc6da01b12cd| ffffffffffff | 0.0.0.0         | 255.255.255.255 | UDP      | 67   |     | 1     | 0     | 0     | 0     | 0       |
| cc6da01b12cd| ffffffffffff | 0.0.0.0         | 255.255.255.255 | UDP      | 68   |     | 1     | 0     | 0     | 0     | 0       |
| 0000ca112233| 14b31f07219e | 104.237.191.1   | 192.168.0.109   | TCP      | 443  |     | 63    | 0     | 0     | 75    | 0       |
| 0000ca112233| 14b31f07219e | 104.237.191.1   | 192.168.0.109   | TCP      | 443  |     | 1     | 0     | 0     | 2     | 0       |
| 0000ca112233| 14b31f07219e | 104.244.46.135  | 192.168.0.109   | TCP      | 443  |     | 0     | 0     | 0     | 9     | 0       |
| 0000ca112233| 14b31f07219e | 104.41.207.73   | 192.168.0.109   | TCP      | 443  |     | 9     | 0     | 0     | 0     | 0       |
| 0000ca112233| 14b31f07219e | 104.43.140.223  | 192.168.0.109   | TCP      | 443  |     | 0     | 0     | 0     | 8     | 0       |
| 0000ca112233| 14b31f07219e | 104.44.88.24    | 192.168.0.109   | TCP      | 443  |     | 0     | 0     | 0     | 20    | 0       |
| 0000ca112233| 14b31f07219e | 104.46.50.125   | 192.168.0.109   | TCP      | 443  |     | 8     | 0     | 0     | 0     | 0       |
| 0000ca112233| 14b31f07219e | 104.92.4.184    | 192.168.0.109   | TCP      | 443  |     | 0     | 0     | 0     | 14    | 0       |
| 000000000000| 000000000000 | 127.0.0.1       | 127.0.1.1       | UDP      | 53   |     | 1224  | 0     | 0     | 687   | 0       |
| 000000000000| 000000000000 | 127.0.1.1       | 127.0.0.1       | UDP      | 53   |     | 1224  | 0     | 0     | 685   | 0       |
| 0000ca112233| 14b31f07219e | 13.107.21.200   | 192.168.0.109   | TCP      | 443  |     | 27    | 0     | 0     | 12    | 0       |
| 0000ca112233| 14b31f07219e | 13.107.3.128    | 192.168.0.109   | TCP      | 443  |     | 131   | 0     | 0     | 55    | 0       |
| 0000ca112233| 14b31f07219e | 13.107.4.52     | 192.168.0.109   | TCP      | 80   |     | 6     | 0     | 0     | 0     | 0       |
| 0000ca112233| 14b31f07219e | 13.107.5.88     | 192.168.0.109   | TCP      | 443  |     | 187   | 0     | 0     | 88    | 0       |
| 0000ca112233| 14b31f07219e | 13.76.219.191   | 192.168.0.109   | TCP      | 443  |     | 0     | 0     | 0     | 7     | 0       |
| 0000ca112233| 14b31f07219e | 13.76.219.210   | 192.168.0.109   | TCP      | 443  |     | 20    | 0     | 0     | 0     | 0       |
| 0000ca112233| 14b31f07219e | 131.253.61.100  | 192.168.0.109   | TCP      | 443  |     | 14    | 0     | 0     | 0     | 0       |
| 0000ca112233| 14b31f07219e | 131.253.61.64   | 192.168.0.109   | TCP      | 443  |     | 34    | 0     | 0     | 0     | 0       |
| 0000ca112233| 14b31f07219e | 131.253.61.68   | 192.168.0.109   | TCP      | 443  |     | 16    | 0     | 0     | 0     | 0       |
| 0000ca112233| 14b31f07219e | 131.253.61.98   | 192.168.0.109   | TCP      | 443  |     | 0     | 0     | 0     | 11    | 0       |
| 0000ca112233| 14b31f07219e | 134.170.58.125  | 192.168.0.109   | TCP      | 443  |     | 92    | 0     | 0     | 0     | 0       |
| 0000ca112233| 14b31f07219e | 137.116.74.190  | 192.168.0.109   | TCP      | 443  |     | 10    | 0     | 0     | 0     | 0       |
| 0000ca112233| 14b31f07219e | 157.56.77.141   | 192.168.0.109   | TCP      | 443  |     | 14    | 0     | 0     | 0     | 0       |
| 0000ca112233| 14b31f07219e | 162.125.16.131  | 192.168.0.109   | TCP      | 443  |     | 4     | 0     | 0     | 0     | 0       |
| 0000ca112233| 14b31f07219e | 162.125.16.5    | 192.168.0.109   | TCP      | 443  |     | 8     | 0     | 0     | 6     | 0       |
| 0000ca112233| 14b31f07219e | 162.125.17.132  | 192.168.0.109   | TCP      | 443  |     | 17    | 0     | 0     | 4     | 0       |
| 0000ca112233| 14b31f07219e | 162.125.17.5    | 192.168.0.109   | TCP      | 443  |     | 12    | 0     | 0     | 12    | 0       |
| 0000ca112233| 14b31f07219e | 162.125.18.133  | 192.168.0.109   | TCP      | 443  |     | 1512  | 0     | 0     | 792   | 0       |
| 0000ca112233| 14b31f07219e | 162.125.32.5    | 192.168.0.109   | TCP      | 443  |     | 125   | 0     | 0     | 79    | 0       |
| 0000ca112233| 14b31f07219e | 67.217.66.244   | 192.168.0.109   | TCP      | 443  |     | 62    | 0     | 0     | 40    | 0       |
| 0000ca112233| 14b31f07219e | 67.217.66.83    | 192.168.0.109   | TCP      | 443  |     | 0     | 0     | 0     | 1     | 0       |
| 0000ca112233| 14b31f07219e | 67.217.93.56    | 192.168.0.109   | TCP      | 443  |     | 0     | 0     | 0     | 1     | 0       |
| 0000ca112233| 14b31f07219e | 68.64.13.250    | 192.168.0.109   | TCP      | 443  |     | 70    | 0     | 0     | 40    | 0       |
| 0000ca112233| 14b31f07219e | 68.64.22.20     | 192.168.0.109   | TCP      | 443  |     | 0     | 0     | 0     | 10    | 0       |
| 0000ca112233| 14b31f07219e | 68.64.23.56     | 192.168.0.109   | TCP      | 443  |     | 0     | 0     | 0     | 1     | 0       |
| 0000ca112233| 14b31f07219e | 68.64.31.56     | 192.168.0.109   | TCP      | 443  |     | 0     | 0     | 0     | 11    | 0       |
| 0000ca112233| 14b31f07219e | 68.64.5.249     | 192.168.0.109   | TCP      | 443  |     | 71    | 0     | 0     | 30    | 0       |
| 0000ca112233| 14b31f07219e | 72.167.218.192  | 192.168.0.109   | TCP      | 995  |     | 2239  | 0     | 0     | 1207  | 0       |
| 0000ca112233| 14b31f07219e | 72.21.91.29     | 192.168.0.109   | TCP      | 80   |     | 3     | 0     | 0     | 3     | 0       |
| 0000ca112233| f80f4142d110 | 74.125.138.136  | 192.168.0.118   | TCP      | 443  |     | 24    | 0     | 0     | 0     | 0       |
| 0000ca112233| f80f4142d110 | 74.125.138.190  | 192.168.0.118   | TCP      | 443  |     | 23    | 0     | 0     | 0     | 0       |
| 0000ca112233| f80f4142d110 | 74.125.21.113   | 192.168.0.118   | TCP      | 443  |     | 21    | 0     | 0     | 0     | 0       |
| 0000ca112233| 14b31f07219e | 74.125.21.121   | 192.168.0.109   | TCP      | 443  |     | 0     | 0     | 0     | 39    | 0       |
| 0000ca112233| f80f4142d110 | 74.125.21.136   | 192.168.0.118   | TCP      | 443  |     | 24    | 0     | 0     | 0     | 0       |
| 0000ca112233| f80f4142d110 | 74.125.21.138   | 192.168.0.118   | TCP      | 443  |     | 0     | 0     | 0     | 24    | 0       |
| 0000ca112233| f80f4142d110 | 74.125.21.91    | 192.168.0.118   | TCP      | 443  |     | 22    | 0     | 0     | 0     | 0       |
| 0000ca112233| 14b31f07219e | 74.125.22.125   | 192.168.0.109   | TCP      | 5222 |     | 593   | 0     | 0     | 356   | 0       |
| 0000ca112233| 14b31f07219e | 74.125.22.125   | 192.168.0.109   | TCP      | 6541 |     | 1     | 0     | 0     | 0     | 0       |
| 0000ca112233| 14b31f07219e | 78.108.117.250  | 192.168.0.109   | TCP      | 443  |     | 72    | 0     | 0     | 40    | 0       |
| 0000ca112233| 14b31f07219e | 78.108.118.250  | 192.168.0.109   | TCP      | 443  |     | 63    | 0     | 0     | 39    | 0       |
| 0000ca112233| 14b31f07219e | 78.108.119.250  | 192.168.0.109   | TCP      | 443  |     | 70    | 0     | 0     | 30    | 0       |
+-------------+--------------+-----------------+-----------------+----------+------+-----+-------+-------+-------+-------+---------+

End Packet Processor
```

Figure 2-9. *Sample output from the PacketRecorder.py script*

Summary

This chapter provides a deep look at the collection, reduction, and mapping of network traffic. The basic methods of capturing and recording observations will be used in future chapters to create a baseline of "normal" operations within an IoT environment. These observations will be used to monitor and detect aberrant behavior and to train machine learning methods.

CHAPTER 3

Raspberry Pi Configuration and PacketRecorder.py Enhancements

When examining a platform for deploying a sensor, there are several key considerations. These considerations typically fall into four broad categories.

1. We must consider the placement of the sensor and the connection to the network that we which wish to sense, such as wired direct connection, traditional 802.11 WIFI, Bluetooth, or other lightweight protocols.

2. We must examine the visibility that can be obtained from the selected network connection and/or the physical location of the sensor. In other words, what network traffic will be visible from a specific vantage point?

© Chet Hosmer 2018
C. Hosmer, *Defending IoT Infrastructures with the Raspberry Pi*,
https://doi.org/10.1007/978-1-4842-3700-7_3

3.   Will multiple sensors be required to derive a
     complete picture of the network that we wish to
     monitor?

4.   Certainly, the cost and long-term viability of the
     platform we intend to deploy need to be considered.

Since this book is focused on using the Raspberry Pi as the sensor, we also need to consider the advantages and limitations of the Pi. We have chosen this platform and the Python programming language based on cost, simplicity, and versatility. Certainly, depending upon the amount of network traffic, along with the speed of the networks that will be monitored, the Pi might not have the performance required. However, since all of the software is written in Python, as more powerful Raspberry Pi or other Linux platforms (small and lightweight or large and high performance) become available, the solution can be scaled to meet the needs.

Basic Configuration (as of This Writing)

We will be using a Raspberry Pi 3 Model B version 1.2 as described back in Chapter 1 and pictured in Figure 1-6 for the examples in the book. We do this to provide a bit more detail on the configuration and to introduce you to the Raspberry Pi and the Raspbian OS commands, which allow us to do a bit of probing.

Note   All the commands executed from the Pi were done from the /home/pi directory. In the default state the default user is pi.

The following line is what the default prompt should look like. Depending on the installation and configuration of your Pi, this might vary slightly.

```
pi@raspberrypi:~ $
```

Note   The ~ (tilde) character is shorthand for the /home/pi directory. Thus, commands are entered directly after the $, allowing you to get some basic but valuable information about your Pi.

Get Information About the Pi CPU

The command retrieves the basic information regarding the Raspberry Pi CPU.

```
pi@raspberrypi:~ $ cat /proc/cpuinfo
```

Note the Pi 3 Model B has four cores. This will become important in later chapters when we utilize the Python multiprocessing library to enhance performance.

```
processor       : 0
model name      : ARMv7 Processor rev 4 (v7l)
BogoMIPS        : 38.40
Features        : half thumb fastmult vfp edsp neon vfpv3 tls
                  vfpv4 idiva idivt vfpd32 lpae evtstrm crc32
CPU implementer : 0x41
CPU architecture: 7
CPU variant     : 0x0
CPU part        : 0xd03
CPU revision    : 4
```

```
processor    : 1
model name   : ARMv7 Processor rev 4 (v7l)
BogoMIPS     : 38.40
Features     : half thumb fastmult vfp edsp neon vfpv3 tls
               vfpv4 idiva idivt vfpd32 lpae evtstrm crc32
CPU implementer : 0x41
CPU architecture: 7
CPU variant  : 0x0
CPU part     : 0xd03
CPU revision : 4

processor    : 2
model name   : ARMv7 Processor rev 4 (v7l)
BogoMIPS     : 38.40
Features     : half thumb fastmult vfp edsp neon vfpv3 tls
               vfpv4 idiva idivt vfpd32 lpae evtstrm crc32
CPU implementer : 0x41
CPU architecture: 7
CPU variant  : 0x0
CPU part     : 0xd03
CPU revision : 4

processor    : 3
model name   : ARMv7 Processor rev 4 (v7l)
BogoMIPS     : 38.40
Features     : half thumb fastmult vfp edsp neon vfpv3 tls
               vfpv4 idiva idivt vfpd32 lpae evtstrm crc32
CPU implementer : 0x41
CPU architecture: 7
CPU variant  : 0x0
CPU part     : 0xd03
CPU revision : 4
```

Get Information Regarding Pi Memory

Another crucial factor regarding the capabilities of the Raspberry Pi is the amount of RAM memory onboard, and more importantly the memory available for use by our application. You can obtain this information using the following command.

pi@raspberrypi:~ $ **get_mem arm**

Notice, unlike the static information regarding the CPU, this is a live report regarding memory usage. As you can see we have a little over 700 MB of fee memory available along with just under 100 MB of free swap memory.

```
Hardware      : BCM2709
Revision      : a02082
Serial        : 0000000093c183ae
MemTotal:        947732 kB
MemFree:         700856 kB
MemAvailable:    796304 kB
Buffers:          20404 kB
Cached:          126088 kB
SwapCached:           0 kB
Active:          129024 kB
Inactive:         84444 kB
Active(anon):     67364 kB
Inactive(anon):   13852 kB
Active(file):     61660 kB
Inactive(file):   70592 kB
Unevictable:          0 kB
Mlocked:              0 kB
SwapTotal:       102396 kB
SwapFree:        102396 kB
```

```
Dirty:                    92 kB
Writeback:                 0 kB
AnonPages:             66816 kB
Mapped:                63560 kB
Shmem:                 14240 kB
Slab:                  16964 kB
SReclaimable:           8312 kB
SUnreclaim:             8652 kB
KernelStack:            1576 kB
PageTables:             2316 kB
NFS_Unstable:              0 kB
Bounce:                    0 kB
WritebackTmp:              0 kB
CommitLimit:          576260 kB
Committed_AS:         721200 kB
VmallocTotal:        1114112 kB
VmallocUsed:               0 kB
VmallocChunk:              0 kB
CmaTotal:               8192 kB
CmaFree:                3724 kB
```

Get Information Regarding the Current Free Memory Only

Digging a bit deeper, this command provides a more targeted result providing us data regarding free memory and the used and free swap space.

pi@raspberrypi:~ $ **free -o -h**

```
              total      used      free    shared    buffers    cached
Mem:           925M      241M      683M       13M        20M      123M
Swap:           99M        0B       99M
```

Get Information Regarding Pi Filesystem

Obtaining information regarding the current active Pi filesystem will help to define the onboard storage we have available.

```
pi@raspberrypi:~ $ df
```

This command provides the information on how the Pi is configured and most importantly how much free space we have available. Performing simple arithmetic (1024 × 8792304; the available blocks × 1K), we see that we have a little over 9 GB available. This make sense as I'm using a 16GB SD Card on this Pi. If you need more space, then you can choose a larger SD Card for your application. Note, the official maximum size is 32GB.

```
Filesystem      1K-blocks     Used Available Use% Mounted on
/dev/root        13606320  4099804   8792304  32% /
devtmpfs           469532        0    469532   0% /dev
tmpfs              473864        0    473864   0% /dev/shm
tmpfs              473864     6460    467404   2% /run
tmpfs                5120        4      5116   1% /run/lock
tmpfs              473864        0    473864   0% /sys/fs/cgroup
/dev/mmcblk0p6      66528    20762     45767  32% /boot
tmpfs               94776        0     94776   0% /run/user/1000
/dev/mmcblk0p5      30701      456     27952   2% /media/pi/
SETTINGS
```

Get Information Regarding USB Devices and Interfaces

We can of course add more storage to the Pi using the available USB expansion slots as well.

I ran this command twice for you. The first is with no external USB devices inserted, and the second is with one added.

```
pi@raspberrypi:~ $ lsusb

Bus 001 Device 004: ID 045e:0745 Microsoft Corp. Nano
Transceiver v1.0 for Bluetooth

Bus 001 Device 003: ID 0424:ec00 Standard Microsystems Corp.
SMSC9512/9514 Fast Ethernet Adapter

Bus 001 Device 002: ID 0424:9514 Standard Microsystems Corp.
Bus 001 Device 001: ID 1d6b:0002 Linux Foundation 2.0 root hub
```

Now, to execute the same command after inserting the external USB SanDisk Cruzer:

```
pi@raspberrypi:~ $ lsusb

Bus 001 Device 004: ID 045e:0745 Microsoft Corp. Nano
Transceiver v1.0 for Bluetooth

Bus 001 Device 005: ID 0781:5406 SanDisk Corp. Cruzer Micro U3

Bus 001 Device 003: ID 0424:ec00 Standard Microsystems Corp.
SMSC9512/9514 Fast Ethernet Adapter
Bus 001 Device 002: ID 0424:9514 Standard Microsystems Corp.
Bus 001 Device 001: ID 1d6b:0002 Linux Foundation 2.0 root hub
```

Get Information About the Version of Linux

This command provides us information about the core version of Linux we are using, but also provides information regarding the current c++ compiler and crosstool that are installed. It is important to keep your Pi updated, including the operating system and development platform.

```
pi@raspberrypi:~ $ cat /proc/version
```

```
Linux version 4.4.50-v7+ (dc4@dc4-XPS13-9333)
(gcc version 4.9.3 (crosstool-NG crosstool-ng-1.22.0-88-g8460611) )
#970 SMP Mon Feb 20 19:18:29 GMT 2017
```

Upgrading Your Pi

Like other more traditional computing platforms, keeping your Pi up to date is an important process. This will ensure that you are running the latest version of software and that security updates are current. In addition, I also update the pip environment for the same reasons (pip is the tool that we use for installing and managing Python packages, such as those found in the Python Package Index.) Here are examples for both:

```
pi@raspberrypi:~ $ sudo apt-get update
```

This will download and install updates to any packages that have updates available (based on the information obtained from the apt-get update command).

```
Get:1 http://mirrordirector.raspbian.org jessie InRelease [14.9 kB]
Get:2 http://archive.raspberrypi.org jessie InRelease [22.9 kB]
Get:3 http://mirrordirector.raspbian.org jessie/main armhf
       Packages [9,536 kB]
Get:4 http://archive.raspberrypi.org jessie/main armhf Packages
       [170 kB]
Get:5 http://archive.raspberrypi.org jessie/ui armhf Packages
       [58.9 kB]
Get:6 http://mirrordirector.raspbian.org jessie/contrib armhf
       Packages [43.3 kB]
```

   ---- Truncated for brevity ----

```
pi@raspberrypi:~ $ sudo apt-get dist-upgrade
```

Using the dist-upgrade will update Pi kernel and firmware.

Finally, as mentioned in the preceding, we need to keep the Python package installer up to date as well, in order to update any third-party Python packages we may use.

```
pi@raspberrypi:~ $ sudo pip install --upgrade pip
```

Important   One final note after executing these updates! You need to reboot the Pi. The command to do that is

```
pi@raspberrypi:~ $ sudo reboot
```

Advancing PacketRecorder.py

Now that we have the Pi configuration in hand, we can begin to advance the baseline of the PacketRecorder.py script we created in Chapter 2. To obtain more interesting information from the packets we see, we need to perform some secondary processing and advanced dictionary of observations. This will allow us to detect and observe packets of interest. Therefore, we are going to make the following enhancements to PacketRecorder.py.

1. Convert port numbers to common port names including known malicious ports

2. Convert MAC addresses to known manufacturers including known suspicious MAC addresses

3. Look up country code based on IP addresses

4. Record the average packet size for each unique connection

5. Update the interface to the PacketRecorder by
    using the built-in argparse library. This will allow
    us to create a command-line interface to the
    PacketRecorder and supply our desired options.

You can always find the latest command-line execution and
parameters by typing the following:

pi@raspberrypi:~/Desktop/RP-10-12-2017 $ **sudo python pr.py -h**

Notice that I moved to the current working directory containing the
PacketRecorder.py source code along with the needed additional support
files. The installation of the full project is available from the source code
for this book. Go to www.apress.com/9781484236994 and click the Source
Code button.

pi@raspberrypi:~/Desktop/RP-10-12-2017 $ **sudo python pr.py -h**
Python Packet Recorder v.85 - Raspberry Pi
Python Forensics, Inc. October 2017
Copyright Python Forensics - All Rights Reserved

usage: Raspberry Pi Packet Recorder V.85 . October 2017 [-h] -m
DURATION

                                                      [-E] [-C]

optional arguments:
  -h, --help   show this help message and exit
  -m DURATION, --duration DURATION
                        specify duration of the recording in minutes
  -E, --ephemeral   if specified ephemeral ports are
considered unique
  -C, --countryReport   if specified a special country report
is generated

57

Step 1: Creating the Lookups

During the examination of observed packets, it is important not to overwhelm that process with significant code, databases, and so on. Remember, the purpose of the PacketRecorder.py application is to create a baseline of a "normal operating" network. This will in fact generate a detailed network device-level asset map for the environment that we are monitoring. This map should be compared to other available device maps (such as those generated by NMAP, administration documentation, etc.).

Thus, our approach is to preprocess lists of known good/bad ports, country codes, and manufacturer indices, and create a fast lookup of those values that can be easily added to the observations dictionary. We can of course generate anomalies identified during the baselining process as well.

Each of the lookups is processed in a comparable manner that starts with the conversion of online data into dictionary objects. We perform this operation as a preprocessing step. Depending upon the complexity of the online data source, the parsing and preparation of these dictionaries can be either simple or quite complex. However, we only perform this preprocessing operation periodically to keep our dictionary lookups up to date.

Once the preprocessing step is complete, we convert the resulting dictionary objects into serialized data (Python pickle files) that are loaded on to the Pi. In this manner the Pi does not require access to the Internet during baselining or operational sensing phases.

To perform this effectively, we extract information from reliable sources:

1. Manufacturer IEEE (Institute of
    Electrical and Electronics Engineers) OUI lists:
    `http://standards-oui.ieee.org/oui.txt`

2. IANA for the known port number/name translations
    `www.iana.org/assignments/service-names-port-`
    `numbers/service-names-port-numbers.xhtml`

3.   Maxmind's Country Location Database `http://dev.maxmind.com/geoip/legacy/geolite/`

Ports Dictionary Creating Example

The following script demonstrates the processing of the IANA text ports list and conversion into a Python dictionary. Once the dictionary is created, the serialization of the dictionary is recorded in the file "ports.pickle".

```
'' Port Dictionary Creation Process '''
'''
Copyright (c) 2017 Python-Forensics and Chet Hosmer, cdh@
python-forensics.org

Permission is hereby granted, free of charge, to any person
obtaining a copy of this software and associated documentation
files (the "Software"), to deal in the Software without
restriction, including without limitation the rights to use,
copy, modify, merge, publish, distribute, sublicense, and/
or sell copies of the Software, and to permit persons to whom
the Software is furnished to do so, subject to the following
conditions:

The above copyright notice and this permission notice shall be
included in all copies or substantial portions of the Software.

'''

''' excerpt from the online ports list
TCP  0   Reserved
TCP  1   Port Service Multiplexer
TCP  2   Management Utility
TCP  3   Compression Process
```

```
TCP   4   Unassigned
TCP   5   Remote Job Entry
'''

import pickle

# Create an Empty Dictionary
portDictionary = {}
records = 0

print "PortList Dictionary Creation Script"
print "Python Forensics, Inc. ver 1.1 2017"
print "Processing PortList.txt"
# Open the PortList Text File
with open("PortList.txt", 'r') as theFile:

    # Process EachLine
    for eachLine in theFile:

        # Create a list of each component of the line
        # Split the line into parts

        lineList = eachLine.split()

        # We need at least three elements to be valid
        # PortType PortNumber  Description
        # The descriptions may be broken up into multiple parts
        of course

        if len(lineList) >= 3:

            # Make the key in the key/value pair

            key = (lineList[1], lineList[0])

            # Determine how many parts we have after type and port
            # We will use this list as the value in the key/value
            pair
```

```
                value = " ".join(lineList[2:])
            # Now create a dictionary entry
            # key = Port,Type
            # Value = Description

            portDictionary[key] = value
            records += 1
        else:
            # if the line does not have the correct number
            # of values skip this line and continue processing
            # the next line
            continue

    # All lines have been processed
    print "Lookup Records Create: ", records
''' Finally we serialize the portDictionary
    for use by PacketRecorder and PacketDetection
    scripts, by creating the file ports.pickle
'''
with open('portTest.pickle', 'wb') as pickleFile:
    pickle.dump(portDictionary, pickleFile)
```

Execution of the Script

To demonstrate the execution of the script, I have copied the source code and PortList.txt file to my local windows system.

Note   The creation of the lookups does not need to be done on the Raspberry Pi; this process can be created on Windows, Linux, or Mac.

When you download the Raspberry Pi installation files from GIT-HUB it will include the required pickle files. Therefore, you will not need to perform this operation. The sample is provided here to explain how the dictionaries are serialized into pickle files (see Listing 3-1).

Listing 3-1. Directory for Execution of the CreatePortPickle.py script

```
c:\ports>dir
 Volume in drive C is OS
 Volume Serial Number is ECD2-7A54

 Directory of c:\ports

10/13/2017  11:22 AM    <DIR>          .
10/13/2017  11:22 AM    <DIR>          ..
10/13/2017  11:17 AM             2,696 CreatePortPickle.py
05/23/2017  08:15 AM           174,165 PortList.txt
               2 File(s)        176,861 bytes
               2 Dir(s)  496,912,228,352 bytes free
```

At this point the script is executed and listing of the resulting directory, which includes the portTest.pickle file.

```
c:\ports>python CreatePortPickle.py

PortList Dictionary Creation Script
Python Forensics, Inc. ver 1.1 2017
Processing PortList.txt
Lookup Records Created:  6367

c:\ports>dir
 Volume in drive C is OS
 Volume Serial Number is ECD2-7A54

 Directory of c:\ports
```

```
10/13/2017   11:27 AM    <DIR>                .
10/13/2017   11:27 AM    <DIR>                ..
10/13/2017   11:17 AM                2,696 CreatePortPickle.py
05/23/2017   08:15 AM              174,165 PortList.txt
10/13/2017   11:27 AM              398,507 portTest.pickle
             3 File(s)            575,368 bytes
             2 Dir(s)   496,910,360,576 bytes free
```

You might notice that the .pickle file is larger than the original PortList. txt file. This is normal, as the keys and internal structure of the dictionary may be larger. However, the efficiency gained through their use in the actual packetRecorder.py script is significant.

Utilizing the Pickle Files in PacketRecorder.py

Integrating the pickle files for is accomplished by creating a class for each lookup type. The initialization (or constructor of the class) loads the associated .pickle file into a dictionary associated with the object. Then a lookup method is included that allows fast lookup of the desired conversion.

- Ethernet Packet Type

- MAC Address to Manufacturer Lookup

- Transport Protocol Lookup

- Port Name Lookup

- Country IP Address Lookup

The following code snippets provide the code for each of the lookup-related classes.

```python
class ETH:

    def __init__(self):
        ''' FrameTypes Supported'''

        self.ethTypes = {}

        with open("ethTypes.pickle2",'rb') as fp:
            self.ethTypes = pickle.load(fp)

    def lookup(self, ethType):
        ''' Returns the FrameType associated with the lookup or
        not=supported'''
        try:
            result = self.ethTypes[ethType]
        except:
            result = "not-supported"

        return result.strip()

# MAC Address Lookup Class
class MAC:

    def __init__(self):
        ''' constructor'''
        # Open the MAC Address OUI Dictionary
        try:
            with open('oui.pickle', 'rb') as pickleFile:
                self.macDict = pickle.load(pickleFile)
        except Exception as err:
            print str(err)

    def lookup(self, macAddress):
        try:
            result = self.macDict[macAddress]
```

```python
            if len(result) >= 2:
                result = ": ".join(result[0:2])
            else:
                result = result[0]
            return result
        except:
            return "unknown"

# Transport Lookup Class

class TRANSPORT:

    def __init__(self):

        # Open the Transport protocol Dictionary
        with open('protocol.pickle', 'rb') as pickleFile:
            self.proDict = pickle.load(pickleFile)

    def lookup(self, protocol):
        try:
            result = self.proDict[protocol]
            return result
        except:
            return ["unknown", "unknown", "unknown"]

#PORTS Lookup Class

class PORTS:

    def __init__(self):

        # Open the Transport protocol Dictionary
        with open('ports.pickle', 'rb') as pickleFile:
            self.portsDict = pickle.load(pickleFile)

    def lookup(self, port, portType):
```

```python
        try:
            lookupValue = (str(port).strip(),portType)
            result = self.portsDict[lookupValue]
            return result
        except:
            return "unknown"

#
# Country Lookup
#

class COUNTRY:

    def __init__(self):

        # download from http://dev.maxmind.com/geoip/legacy/
        geolite/
        self.giv4 = pygeoip.GeoIP('geoIPv4.dat')
        self.giv6 = pygeoip.GeoIP('geoIPv6.dat')

    def lookup(self, ipAddr, kind):

        try:
            if kind == 'IPv4':
                return self.giv4.country_name_by_addr(ipAddr)
            elif kind == 'IPv6':
                return self.giv6.country_name_by_addr(ipAddr)
            else:
                return ''
        except:
            return ''
```

Instantiating and Accessing the Lookup Methods

The next step is to instantiate each of the classes into locally useable objects and then use the associated lookup functions when processing the observed packet.

Note   We perform this instantiation as part of the packetProcessor Class constructor, so the lookup methods are available during packet processing.

Code Snippet to Instantiate the Classes into Objects

```
class PacketProcessor:
    """

    Packet Processor Class Methods
    __init__  Constructor
    PacketProcessor(self, packet) : processes a single packet
    PrintMap(self) : prints out the content of the map
    """

    def __init__(self):
        """"Constructor"""
        '''

        Create Lookup Objects

        These Object provide lookups for:
        Ethernet Frame Types
        MAC Addresses
        Transport Protocol Types
        TCP/UDP Port Names
        Country
        '''

        self.traOBJ  = TRANSPORT()
        self.ethOBJ  = ETH()
        self.portOBJ = PORTS()
```

```
self.ouiOBJ  = MAC()
self.cc      = COUNTRY()
```

Using the Lookups During Packet Processing

Now that the objects self.traOBJ, self.ethOB, self.portOBJ, self.ouiOBJ, and self.cc have been created, we can put them to use during normal packet processing. I have chosen to depict a couple of these here to give an example of how they are utilized.

Sample IPv4 Processing Conversion (Excerpt)

This excerpt depicts the conversion of the source and destination IP addresses into country location and converts the protocol number of the IPv4 packet into the associated country name.

```
# covert the source and destination address to typical dotted
notation strings
        self.packetSize = packetLength
        self.srcIP = socket.inet_ntoa(sourceIP);
        self.dstIP = socket.inet_ntoa(destIP);

        self.srcCC = self.cc.lookup(self.srcIP, 'IPv4')
        self.dstCC = self.cc.lookup(self.dstIP, 'IPv4')

        translate = self.traOBJ.lookup(str(protocol))
        transProtocol = translate[0]
```

Convert the Port Numbers into Port Names (Excerpt)

```
# unpack the TCP Header to obtain the
# source and destination port
        tcpHeaderBuffer = struct.unpack('!HHLLBBHHH' ,
        stripTCPHeader)
```

```
        self.srcPort = tcpHeaderBuffer[0]
        self.dstPort = tcpHeaderBuffer[1]

        self.srcPortName = self.portOBJ.lookup(self.
        srcPort, 'TCP')
        self.dstPortName = self.portOBJ.lookup(self.
        dstPort, 'TCP')
```

Executing the Updated PacketRecorder.py

In each chapter, as we advance and integrate new capabilities into PacketRecorder.py baselining capability, and into the ultimate sensor, I will be providing sample output from the latest version.

Note   that the name of the PacketRecorder.py was changed to pr.py for simplicity.

```
    pi@raspberrypi:~/Desktop/RP-10-12-2017 $ sudo python
pr.py -m 1 -C
```
The command line requests that pr.py execute for 1 minute using the -m option. The -C option requests that a separate country report be generated.

Script Execution

In this run you can see new columns in the report that include

1. Port Name

2. Manufacturer

3. Average Packet Size

In addition, near the bottom you can see that IPv6 packet captures are now included (Figure 3-1).

```
pi@raspberrypi:~/Desktop/RP-10-12-2017 $ sudo python pr.py -m 1 -C
Python Packet Recorder v.85 - Raspberry Pi
Python Forensics, Inc.  October 2017
Copyright Python Forensics - All Rights Reserved

| Promiscuous Mode Enabled for eth0
Packet Processor    : Ready;

Record Complete - Printing Results
```

Alert	SrcMac	DstMac	FrameType	SrcIP	DstIP	Prot.Op	Port	PortName	-->	MFG	CC	Avg-PacketSize	12AVb	06AVb	12MPb	06PPb	WEEKEND
	000CA112233	010B5E7FFFFA	IPV4	192.168.0.1	239.255.255.250	UDP	3540	UPnP SSDP		unknown		372	0	1	0	0	0
	000CA112233	14B31F97219E	IPV4	157.56.149.60	192.168.0.119	TCP	443			US: ARRIS	United States	91	0	3	0	0	0
	000CA112233	14B31F97219E	IPV4	162.125.18.133	192.168.0.119	TCP	443	HTTP proto		US: ARRIS	United States	26	0	5	0	0	0
	000CA112233	14B31F97219E	IPV4	162.125.18.133	192.168.0.119	TCP	11801	unknown		US: Dell I		40	0	1	0	0	0
	000CA112233	14B31F97219E	IPV4	162.125.18.133	192.168.0.119	TCP	15917	unknown		US: Dell I		40	0	1	0	0	0
	000CA112233	14B31F97219E	IPV4	162.125.34.129	192.168.0.119	TCP	443	HTTP proto		US: ARRIS	United States	20	0	15	0	0	0
	000CA112233	14B31F97219E	IPV4	162.125.34.129	192.168.0.119	TCP	13823	unknown		US: Dell I		40	0	1	0	0	0
	000CA112233	14B31F97219E	IPV4	162.125.34.129	192.168.0.119	TCP	16013	unknown		US: Dell I		40	0	1	0	0	0
	000CA112233	14B31F97219E	IPV4	162.125.6.3	192.168.0.119	TCP	16073	unknown		US: ARRIS		297	0	2	0	0	0
	000CA112233	14B31F97219E	IPV4	162.125.6.3	192.168.0.119	TCP	443	HTTP proto		US: Dell I	United States	55	0	1	0	0	0
	000CA112233	14B31F97219E	IPV4	172.217.11.133	192.168.0.119	TCP	15990	unknown		US: Dell I	United States	52	0	1	0	0	0
	000CA112233	14B31F97219E	IPV4	172.217.11.133	192.168.0.119	TCP	443	HTTP proto		US: Dell I		52	0	1	0	0	0
	000CA112233	14B31F97219E	IPV4	204.79.197.213	192.168.0.119	TCP	15904	unknown		US: ARRIS	United States	40	0	2	0	0	0
	000CA112233	14B31F97219E	IPV4	204.79.197.213	192.168.0.119	TCP	443	HTTP proto		US: Dell I		40	0	1	0	0	0
	000CA112233	14B31F97219E	IPV4	209.18.47.62	192.168.0.119	UDP	15821	unknown		US: ARRIS	United States	103	0	10	0	0	0
	000CA112233	14B31F97219E	IPV4	209.18.47.62	192.168.0.119	UDP	53	Domain Nam		US: ARRIS	United States	40	0	1	0	0	0
	000CA112233	14B31F97219E	IPV4	74.125.138.125	192.168.0.119	TCP	5222	Jabber Ser		US: Dell I	United States	40	0	6	0	0	0
	000CA112233	14B31F97219E	IPV4	74.125.138.125	192.168.0.119	TCP	22613	unknown		US: ARRIS		52	0	10	0	0	0
	000CA112233	14B31F97219E	IPV4	74.125.138.188	192.168.0.119	UDP	5228	unknown		US: Dell I	United States	7	0	2	0	0	0
	000CA112233	14B31F97219E	IPV4	74.125.196.189	192.168.0.119	UDP	443	unknown		US: ARRIS	United States	244	0	1	0	0	0
	000CA112233	34172856A5E7	IPV4	209.18.47.61	192.168.0.123	UDP	53	Domain Nam		US: ARRIS	United States	244	0	1	0	0	0
	000CA112233	34172856A5E7	IPV4	23.217.38.56	192.168.0.123	TCP	443	HTTP proto		US: Dell I	United States	98	0	1	0	0	0
	000CA112233	34172856A5E7	IPV4	40.69.223.198	192.168.0.123	TCP	7001	WebLogic S		US: ARRIS	Ireland	10	0	1	0	0	0
	000CA112233	AEC0A5FA0552	IPV4	209.133.212.170	192.168.0.109	TCP	39214	unknown		unknown	United States	130	0	1	0	0	0
	000CA112233	AEC0A5FA0552	IPV4	209.133.212.170	239.255.255.250	UDP	1900	UPnP SSDP		unknown		220	0	1	0	0	0
	000C8A979036	010B5E7FFFFA	IPV4	192.168.0.107	239.255.255.250	UDP	44693	unknown		unknown		352	0	1	0	0	0
	000C8A979036	010B5E7FFFFA	IPV4	192.168.0.107	239.255.255.250	UDP		unknown		US: Bose C	United States	155	0	1	0	0	0

Alert	SrcMac	DstMac	FrameType	SrcIP	DstIP	Prot.Op	Port	PortName	-->	MFG	CC	Avg-PacketSize	12AVb	06AVb	12MPb	06PPb	WEEKEND
	A86G7F20CBC1	FFFFFFFFFFFF	IPV4	192.168.0.100	192.168.0.255	UDP	17500	unknown		unknown		228	0	1	0	0	0
	A86G7F20CBC1	FFFFFFFFFFFF	IPV4	192.168.0.100	255.255.255.255	UDP	17500	unknown		unknown		228	0	1	0	0	0
	AECA05FA0552	000CA112233	IPV4	192.168.0.109	209.133.212.170	UDP	39214	WebLogic S		unknown	United States	40	0	1	0	0	0
	BCA02A0A59AE	010B5E5D0000B	IPV4	192.168.0.115	224.0.0.251	UDP	5353	unknown		unknown		142	0	2	0	0	0
	CCGOA0101ZCD	010B5EC7FFFFA	IPV4	192.168.0.124	239.255.255.250	UDP	1900	UPnP SSDP		unknown		306	0	1	0	0	0
	4C74GF729GF7	3333000000FB	IPV6	fe80::18ac:3003:bc97:86dc	ff02::fb	UDP	5353	unknown		unknown		37	0	1	0	0	0
	5CF7E67060KC6	3333000000FB	IPV6	fe80::435:a36b:9f1a:c2a8	ff02::fb	UDP	5353	unknown		unknown		160	0	1	0	0	0
	BCA02A0A59AE	3333000000FB	IPV6	fe80::1a93f:8ca9:eef5:5cb5	ff02::fb	UDP	5353	unknown		unknown		122	0	1	0	0	0

Figure 3-1. Packer recorder

Foreign Country Hits (Outside the United States)

An additional report is also generated that extracts any foreign countries that were detected based on the IP address translation (Figure 3-2).

Alert	srcMac	DstMac	FrameType	SrcIP	DstIP	Prot.Op	Port	-->	PortName	MFG	CC	Avg-PacketSize	12AM>	06AM>	12PM>	06PM>	WEEKEND
	0000CA112233	14B31F07219E	IPV4	202.173.28.250	192.168.0.119	TCP	443		HTTP proto	US: ARRIS	Australia	4	0	10	0	0	0
	0000CA112233	14B31F07219E	IPV4	54.153.230.99	192.168.0.119	TCP	443		HTTP proto	US: ARRIS	Australia	4	0	10	0	0	0
	14B31F07219E	0000CA112233	IPV4	192.168.0.119	202.173.28.250	TCP	443		HTTP proto	US: ARRIS	Australia	40	0	1	0	0	0
	14B31F07219E	0000CA112233	IPV4	192.168.0.119	54.153.230.99	TCP	443		HTTP proto	US: ARRIS	Australia	40	0	1	0	0	0
	0000CA112233	3417EB56A5E7	IPV4	185.189.92.231	192.168.0.123	TCP	443		HTTP proto	US: ARRIS	Czech Republic	52	0	2	0	0	0
	3417EB56A5E7	0000CA112233	IPV4	192.168.0.123	185.189.92.231	TCP	443		HTTP proto	US: ARRIS	Czech Republic	41	0	1	0	0	0
	0000CA112233	14B31F07219E	IPV4	78.108.118.250	192.168.0.119	TCP	443		HTTP proto	US: ARRIS	Europe	4	0	10	0	0	0
	14B31F07219E	0000CA112233	IPV4	192.168.0.119	78.108.118.250	TCP	443		HTTP proto	US: ARRIS	Europe	40	0	1	0	0	0
	0000CA112233	3417EB56A5E7	IPV4	40.69.223.198	192.168.0.123	TCP	443		HTTP proto	US: ARRIS	Ireland	8	0	11	0	0	0
	0000CA112233	3417EB56A5E7	IPV4	52.169.123.48	192.168.0.123	TCP	443		HTTP proto	US: ARRIS	Ireland	8	0	11	0	0	0
	3417EB56A5E7	0000CA112233	IPV4	192.168.0.123	40.69.223.198	TCP	443		HTTP proto	US: ARRIS	Ireland	40	0	1	0	0	0
	3417EB56A5E7	0000CA112233	IPV4	192.168.0.123	52.169.123.48	TCP	443		HTTP proto	US: ARRIS	Ireland	40	0	1	0	0	0

Figure 3-2. *Foreign country report*

Summary

This chapter provided an examination of the Raspberry Pi using several special Raspbian Pi command-line tools. We also considered both the advantages and some potential limitations of the Pi based on available memory and filesystem space.

We added some finishing touches to the baselining script PacketRecorder.py, including the following:

- Ethernet packet type
- MAC address to manufacturer lookup
- Transport protocol lookup
- Port name lookup
- Country IP address lookup
- Recording of IPv6 packets
- Recording of ARP packets
- Recording of average packet size observed for each unique connection
- Finally, a command-line execution that directs the execution of the script

We also added a second report option for generating a report relating to country IP addresses outside the United States. In the next version, we will add an allowed/blacklisted country list to generate even more data regarding the external connections made.

In Chapter 4, we will develop the sensor script, which will utilize a prerecorded baseline (generated by PacketRecorder) and report on anomalies between the baseline and the live environment. We will also generate a specific report that isolates IoT-based protocol observations versus other network traffic.

CHAPTER 4

Raspberry Pi as a Sensor

Moving from a packet recorder to a packet sensor requires us to examine the differences between the activity that was observed during the recording period versus the active monitoring for aberrant behavior.

Turning the Packet Recorder into a Sensor

As we advance the PacketRecorder into a complete sensor platform that can monitor a live network and report anomalies, several major enhancements need to be made. These enhancements will make it easier to

1. Operate the recorder and sensor using the same interface.

2. Generate HTML reports that cover the following:

   a. Overall master report

   b. Observed MAC addresses/manufacturers

   c. Observed country connections

   d. Observed port usage

   e. Observed possible IoT connections

© Chet Hosmer 2018
C. Hosmer, *Defending IoT Infrastructures with the Raspberry Pi*,
https://doi.org/10.1007/978-1-4842-3700-7_4

    f.   Observed possible industrial control system (ICS) connections

    g.   Alerts generated during sensor mode

3.   Provide basic status information directly on the Raspberry Pi.

4.   Finally, produce the recorder/sensor as a single executable file.

Raspberry Pi Sensor/Recorder Design

As you can see in Figure 4-1, the major operational elements of the design include an event-driven GUI (Graphical User Interface), completely developed in native Python, using the TKinter standard library. This adheres to our goal of keeping the code base small and portable. This ensures compatibility with new Raspberry Pi devices as they progress.

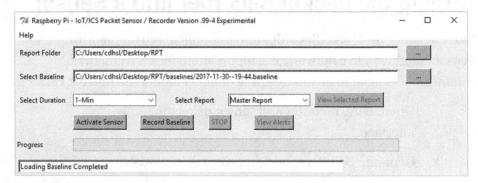

Figure 4-1. *Snapshot of the Raspberry Pi sensor/recorder GUI*

In addition, a real-time ePaper display was added (as an optional element) to the Raspberry Pi itself (Figure 4-2). This provides feedback directly from the Raspberry Pi in both recording and monitoring modes. More information regarding the PaPirus ePaper display is available from the manufacturer at `www.pi-supply.com/product/papirus-epaper-eink-screen-hat-for-raspberry-pi/`.

Figure 4-2. *Raspberry Pi configured with a PaPirus real-time display*

Design Overview

Figure 4-3 depicts the overall operational design of the Pi sensor/recorder.

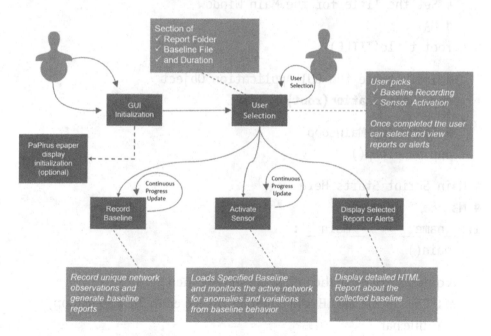

Figure 4-3. *Raspberry Pi sensor/recorder*

The Pi sensor/recorder is set up to execute within an event-driven application loop supported by Python and TKinter.

The main code section is established as follows:

```
# Script Constants
# M1
NAME    = "Raspberry Pi - IoT/ICS Packet Sensor / Recorder"
VERSION = " Version .99-4 Experimental "
TITLE   = NAME+'\t'+VERSION

# Initialize the root TK Window
# M2from Tkinter import *
root = Tk()

def main():

    # Set the Title for the Main Window
    # M3
    root.title(TITLE)

    # Instantiate the GUI Application Object
    app = Application(root)

    # Start App MainLoop
    app.mainloop()

# Main Script Starts Here
# M3
if __name__ == '__main__':
    main()
```

A quick overview of the initialization is defined here:

M1: Creates the TITLE constant to be displayed in the application window title bar.

7⁄4 Raspberry Pi - IoT/ICS Packet Sensor / Recorder Version .99-4 Experimental   —   □   ×

M2: Imports the TKinter Python library and instantiates a new TK object. This will be used as the main window object and event handler in the application.

M3: The main takeaway here is the highlighted call that initializes the application by passing in the root object instantiated from TK.

Next, we'll look at this application handler and the list of methods that have been created to control the distinct aspects of the application.

```python
class Application(Frame):
    ''' APPLICATION CLASS GUI FRAME USING Tkinter '''
    def __init__(self, master=None):

        # Define the instance variables to be
        # collected from the GUI
        # A1
        self.folderSelection   = ''
        self.baselineSelection = ''
        self.baselineGood      = False
        self.reportFolderGood  = False
        self.abortFlag         = False
        self.baselineCC  = {}
        self.baselineMAC = {}

        # Create the basic frame
        # A2
        Frame.__init__(self, master)
        self.parent = master

        # Initialize the GUI
        self.initUI()

        # Initialize PaPirus if available
        # A3
        if PA_ON:
            self.paObj = PA()
```

Examining the main sections of the application class, we find three main sections:

A1: Establishes object attributes that will be associated with each instantiation of the application class. For example, variables that hold state information regarding the baseline and report selections are initialized here, along with dictionaries that will be used by the sensor during monitoring activities. For example, the baselineCC dictionary will hold countries that were observed during the recording phase. Then any new country observations that are observed during the sensor stage can be reported as anomalous.

A2: Creates the parent window frame that will be used by the application. Most importantly, the initUI() method is called; this establishes all the GUI widgets on the window, such as labels, buttons, text boxes, drop-down lists, progress bars, status displays, and menu options.

In the next section we will take a look at the list of methods that have been created and examine a couple of those in detail.

A3: Finally, if a PaPirus display was attached and detected, an object is instantiated to handle the interface with the display. We will see how this is done later in this chapter.

Now let's take a 30,000-foot view of the methods that have been created to handle the user interface and perform the defined functions. At this point we are just looking at the methods that have been defined as shown in Figure 4-4 and Table 4-1.

```
def btnSelectFile(self):
# Handle Folder Browse Button Click

def btnSelectFolder(self):
def btnSelectBaseLine(self):
def btnViewSelectedReport(self):
def btnViewAlerts(self):
def btnActivateSensor(self):
def btnPerformCapture(self):
def SaveOb(self, d):
def GenCSV(self, d):
def GenHTML(self, d):
def GenCOUNTRY(self, d):
def GenICS(self, d):
def GenIOT(self, d):
def GenMFG(self, d):
def GenPortUsage(self, d):
def translateAlertCodes(self, alerts):
def GenAlerts(self, d):
'''
def btnSTOPCapture(self):
def menuToolsExit(self, event=True):
'''
def menuAbout(self, event=True):
```

Figure 4-4. *Application object methods*

Brief descriptions of the application object methods are given in Table 4-1.

Table 4-1. *GUI method definitions*

Method	Description
initUI	Creates and initializes all the display widgets found on the application frame. Once all the widgets are created, the lookup tables used by the application are loaded and the status bar is updated.
btnSelectFolder	Handles the button click to the right of the Report Folder selection and provides a folder browser for the user. The user must select an existing folder, or create a new folder to store the results of the record baseline or activate sensor selections.
btnSelectBaseline	Handles the selection of an existing baseline that will be used in sensor mode to detect anomalies from the recorded baseline, for example, new connections, devices, port usage and countries contacted.
btnPerformCapture	Begins the record baseline process. Based on the selected duration, this method will run to completion unless interrupted by the stop button. Note: this button will not be active until a report folder has been selected.
btnActivateSensor	Utilizes the selected baseline and begins the process of monitoring network activity and comparing those results to the baseline. Like the btnPerformCapture method, it will run for the selected duration unless interrupted by the stop button. Note: this button will not be active until a report folder has been selected along with a valid baseline.

(continued)

Table 4-1. (*continued*)

Method	Description
btnStopCapture	Activated upon pressing the stop button during a baseline recording or sensor execution. It will interrupt the recording or sensor, but will store the intermediate results. Note: this button will only be activated during baseline recording or sensor monitoring activity.
btnViewSelectedReport	Displays the report currently selected by the user in the Select Report drop-down menu. Possible reports include the following: Master report Manufacturer report (OUI device name) Country report Port usage report IoT report ICS report
btnViewAlerts	Activated by the user pressing the view alerts button. This button is only active after a sensor execution has been completed. The method will display the current alert report generated by the last sensor operation.

The next set of methods perform operations upon completing the recording of a baseline. The method uses the unique dictionary created during the baseline recording process.

SaveOB	Saves the baseline as a serialized Python pickle object. The baseline is saved in the baseline directory that is created under the selected report folder.

(*continued*)

Table 4-1. (*continued*)

Method	Description
GenCSV	Generates a comma-separated value (CSV) file in the reports folder. The CSV contains all the unique observations during the record baseline process.
GenHTML	Generates the master HTML report
GenCountry	Generates the country HTML report
GenICS	Generates the possible ICS observed activity HTML report
GenIoT	Generates the possible IoT observed activity HTML report
GenMFG	Generates the observed manufacturers HTML report
GenPortUsage	Generates the PortUsage HTML report
translateAlertCodes	Converts alert codes generated by the Pi sensor into meaningful messages
GenAlerts	Generates the alerts HTML report generated by the sensor operation
btnStopCapture	Allows the user to stop the recording or sensor, but still generate the reports
MenuAbout	Displays the application about box
MenuToolsExit	Handles the exiting of the MenuTools

Method Details

Next, we will take a deeper look at some of the key methods defined here.

Note   A complete listing of the completed Python solutions is available in the Appedix A, provides instructions on accessing the source code.

Initializing the GUI (initUI)

```python
def initUI(self):

    # Create Menu Bar
    # U1
    menuBar = Menu(self.parent)  # menu begin
    toolsMenu = Menu(menuBar, tearoff=0)
    toolsMenu.add_command(label='About', accelerator='Ctrl+A',
        command=self.menuAbout, underline=0)

    toolsMenu.add_separator()

    toolsMenu.add_command(label='Exit', accelerator='Ctrl+X',
        command=self.menuToolsExit)

    menuBar.add_cascade(label='Help', menu=toolsMenu,
    underline=0)
    self.parent.config(menu=menuBar)  # menu ends

    self.bind_all("<Control-x>", self.menuToolsExit)
    self.bind_all("<Control-a>", self.menuAbout)

    # Folder Selection
    # U2
    self.lblReport = Label(self.parent, anchor='w',
    text="Report Folder")
    self.lblReport.grid(row=1, column=0, padx=5, pady=10,
    sticky='w')
    self.ReportFolder = Label(self.parent, anchor='w', bd=3, bg
    = 'white', fg='black',width=80, relief=SUNKEN)
    self.ReportFolder.grid(row=1, column=1, padx=5, pady=0,
    sticky='w')
```

```
self.buttonReportFolder = Button(self.parent, text=' ... ',
    command=self.btnSelectFolder, width=5, bg ='gray',
    fg='black',
    activebackground='black', activeforeground='green')
self.buttonReportFolder.grid(row=1, column=1, padx=585,
pady=0, sticky='w')

self.lblBaseline = Label(self.parent, anchor='w',
text="Select Baseline")
self.lblBaseline.grid(row=2, column=0, padx=5, pady=10,
sticky='w')
self.fileBaseline = Label(self.parent, anchor='w', bd=3,
bg = 'white', fg='black',width=80, relief=SUNKEN)
self.fileBaseline.grid(row=2, column=1, padx=5, pady=0,
sticky='w')
self.buttonSelectBaseline = Button(self.parent,
text=' ... ',
command=self.btnSelectBaseLine, width=5, bg ='gray',
fg='black',
activebackground='black', activeforeground='green')
self.buttonSelectBaseline.grid(row=2, column=1, padx=585,
pady=0,
            sticky='w')

# Specify the Duration of the Scan
# U3
self.lblDuration = Label(self.parent, anchor='w',
text="Select Duration")
self.lblDuration.grid(row=3, column=0, padx=5, pady=10,
sticky='w')
self.durationValue = StringVar()
self.duration = ttk.Combobox(self.parent,
        textvariable=self.durationValue)
```

```
self.duration['values'] = ('1-Min', '10-Min', '30-Min',
'1-Hr', '4-Hr', '8-Hr', '12-Hr', '18-Hr', '1-Day', '2-Day',
'4-Day', '7-Day','2-Week', '4-Week')
self.duration.current(0)
self.duration.grid(row=3, column=1, padx=5, pady=10,
sticky='w')

# Capture Packet Button
# U4 Action Buttons
self.ActivateSensor = Button(self.parent, text='Activate
Sensor',
        command=self.btnActivateSensor, bg ='gray',
        fg='black',
        activebackground='black', activeforeground='green')

self.ActivateSensor.grid(row=8, column=1, padx=5, pady=5,
sticky=W)
self.ActivateSensor['state']=DISABLED

self.CapturePackets = Button(self.parent, text='Record
Baseline',
        command=self.btnPerformCapture, bg ='gray',
        fg='black',
        activebackground='black', activeforeground='green')

self.CapturePackets.grid(row=8, column=1, padx=120, pady=5,
sticky=W)
self.CapturePackets['state']=DISABLED

self.StopCapture = Button(self.parent, text='STOP',
        command=self.btnSTOPCapture, bg ='gray',
        fg='black',
```

```
        activebackground='black', activeforeground='green')

self.StopCapture.grid(row=8, column=1, padx=240, pady=5,
sticky=W)
self.StopCapture['state']=DISABLED

self.ViewAlerts = Button(self.parent, text='View Alerts',
        command=self.btnViewAlerts, bg ='gray', fg='black',
        activebackground='black', activeforeground='green')

self.ViewAlerts.grid(row=8, column=1, padx=320, pady=5,
sticky=W)
self.ViewAlerts['state']=DISABLED

# SETUP a Progress Bar
```

 # U5 Progress Bar Setup

```
self.progressLabel = Label(self.parent, anchor='w',
text="Progress")
self.progressLabel.grid(row=9, column=0, padx=0, pady=10,
sticky='w')
self.progressBar = ttk.Progressbar(self.parent,
orient='horizontal',
        mode='determinate')

self.progressBar.grid(row=9, column=1, padx=5, pady=10,
sticky='w')

# Special Code to align the width of the progress bar
colWidth = self.ReportFolder.winfo_width()
self.progressBar['length'] = colWidth
self.update()
```

```python
# Report Setup
# U6 Reporting
self.lblReport = Label(self.parent, anchor='w', text="
Select Report")
self.lblReport.grid(row=3, column=1, padx=175, pady=10,
sticky='w')
self.ReportSelection = StringVar()

self.report = ttk.Combobox(self.parent, textvariable=self.
ReportSelection)

self.report['values'] = ('Master Report', 'MFG Report',
'Country Report', 'Port Usage Report', 'ICS Report', 'IoT
Report')

self.report.current(0)
self.report.grid(row=3, column=1, padx=275, pady=10,
sticky='w')

# View Report
self.viewReport = Button(self.parent, text='View
Selected Report', command=self.btnViewSelectedReport,
bg ='gray', fg='black', activebackground='black',
activeforeground='green')

self.viewReport.grid(row=3, column=1, padx=425, pady=5,
sticky=W)
self.viewReport['state']=DISABLED

# Status Message
# U7 Status Bar

self.statusText = Label(self.parent, anchor='w', width=80,
bd=3, bg ='white', fg='black', relief=SUNKEN)
```

87

```
self.statusText.grid(row=10, column=0, columnspan=2,
padx=5, pady=5, sticky='w')

self.update()
```

Defining a GUI in Python can be accomplished with many different third-party libraries. However, here we have chosen to utilize the built-in Python TKinter Library, TK for short. Tk/Tcl is an integral component of standard Python. It provides a robust and platform independent windowing toolkit that is readily available to Python programmers using the TKinter module, and its extensions. The extensions include the Tix and ttk modules. Additional details regarding TKinter can be found in the Python Standard Library at https://docs.python.org/2/library/tk.html.

The TKinter module is a thin object-oriented layer on top of Tcl/Tk, which provides a set of wrappers that implement the Tk widgets as Python classes. In addition, the internal module _TKinter provides a threadsafe mechanism which allows Python and Tcl to interact.

Using TKinter requires us to make specific declarations and configurations for each of the onscreen widgets along with any event handlers (for example button clicks) for each widget.

Configuring TK can be done using one of two geometry-based methods, commonly referred to as *Grid* and *Pack*. We have chosen to use the Grid method. Using the Grid method organizes widgets in a table-like structure, where each widget (buttons, labels, combo boxes, progress bars, etc.) are then placed at a specific row and column location.

In addition to visual widgets, other objects such as menu-based objects like those declared in the U1 highlighted section are placed on the frames menu bar.

In order to better explain how this is done, we will walk through each code section U1 through U7.

U1-Menu Bar

This section declares the simple menu item "Help" that contains just three items:

1. About

2. A horizontal separator line

3. Exit

In addition, the keyboard shortcut bindings for *Ctrl-X* and *Ctrl-A* are defined to allow keystroke menu selections.

Finally, specific command executions are associated with the ***About*** and ***Exit*** menu options. For example:

```
command=self.menuAbout
command=self.menuToolsExit
```

If you examine Table 4-1 you will see the declarations for these two methods as part of the application object. We will examine those methods later in this chapter.

This produces the menu as shown in Figure 4-5.

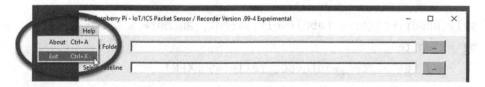

Figure 4-5. *Menu bar illustration*

U2-Folder and File Selection

The folder selection code section defines two selections, and each selection contains three widgets:

1. A label widget that indicates the name of the field

2. A sunken label that will hold the resulting user selection

3. A button to launch the requisite folder and file selection dialogs

Taking a close look at the first folder selection, we first define the label widget with the text **Report Folder** and place that label at row 1, column 0 on the parent frame and we anchor the frame to the westmost position in the column.

```
self.lblReport = Label(self.parent, anchor='w',
text="Report Folder")
self.lblReport.grid(row=1, column=0, padx=5, pady=10, sticky='w')
```

Next, we specify another label widget at row 1, column 1 and specify the label to be sunken to represent data that is specified.

```
self.ReportFolder = Label(self.parent, anchor='w', bd=3,
bg = 'white',
        fg='black',width=80, relief=SUNKEN)

self.ReportFolder.grid(row=1, column=1, padx=5, pady=0, sticky='w')
```

Finally, we add a button widget at row 1, column 2 that will launch a dialog box for the user to select the folder where reports, baseline, and alerts will be stored. Notice this widget has a command associated with *self.btnSelectFolder*. This method is also defined in Table 4-1, and again, we will examine the details of this method. The method source code is shown here.

```
self.buttonReportFolder = Button(self.parent, text=' ... ',
        command=self.btnSelectFolder, width=5, bg ='gray',
        fg='black',
        activebackground='black', activeforeground='green')
self.buttonReportFolder.grid(row=1, column=1, padx=585, pady=0,
        sticky='w')
```

U3-Duration Selection

Duration selection specifies two widgets. The first is a label to display "Select Duration", and the second is a combo box to list the possible duration options available. The label is placed at row 3, column 0, while the combo box is placed at row 3, column 1. When the user clicks the combo box, the list of possible options is displayed as shown in Figure 4-6. The current selection is maintained by the widget and we can retrieve that selection at any time. Of course, the string value will have to have been converted into a useable time value.

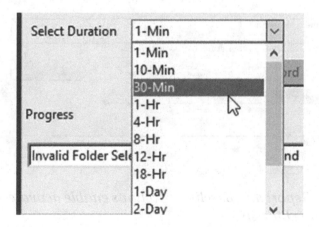

Figure 4-6. *Duration selection*

U4-Action Buttons

The action buttons, activate sensor, record baseline, stop and view Alerts are defined here. They are all defined to be placed in row 8, column 1. However, each contains a different padx value (padding from the westmost position of the row) allowing the buttons to be separated. Without the padding, they would be displayed on top of each other.

In addition, each button has a defined command associated with it that will be executed when pressed.

Also, notice that each of the buttons is set to DISABLED. The rationale is that the buttons cannot activate the specific operations until the report folder and/or the baseline have been correctly selected.

In addition, the stop button will be enabled once either the activate sensor or record baseline operations are underway, allowing the user to interrupt the operations. Once the selections have been made the buttons become activated, as shown in Figure 4-7.

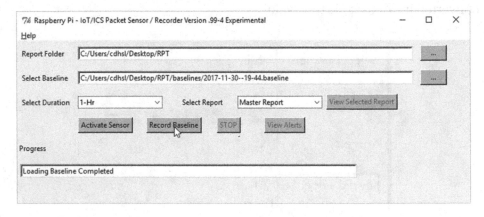

Figure 4-7. *Report and baseline selections enable activate sensor and record baseline buttons*

The source code for each button selection are covered in the GUI Source Code Selection.

U5-Progress Bar

When the activate sensor or record baseline process is underway, a progress bar will be displayed to depict the time remaining in the scan. For this widget we are using a label and a ttk progress bar widget.

U6-Report Selection

As with the duration selection widgets, we are using a combo box to provide a list of possible reports that can be selected, a label to display the text "Select Report", and a button to display the selected report. Note that the view selected report button is also disabled during initialization and only enabled when reports are available for display, as shown in Figure 4-8.

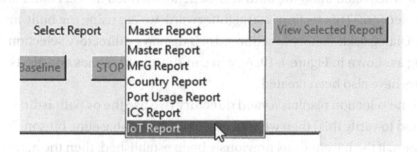

Figure 4-8. *Select report section*

U7-Status Bar

The last section defines the status bar at the bottom of the frame. This is used to report status as the application executes. Once again, we use a simple sunken label widget for the status bar (Figure 4-9). The widget is placed at row 10, column 0.

Figure 4-9. *Application status bar*

93

Exploring Other Application Methods

Now that we have initialized the application interface, let's look at the underlying functions that perform operations based on the user interactions described in Figure 4-3. We will start with selection of the report folder and baseline. The application will write newly generated reports to the selected report folder. In addition, the subfolders **Baselines** and **Alerts** will be created to hold any recorded baselines and alerts generated during active sensor operation.

Selecting the Report Folder (btnSelectFolder)

Start with the btnSelectFolder method (depicted in code segment F1), which is activated upon the button click action defined in "U2 Folder and File Selection." This section is straightforward; we are using the built-in tkFileDialog.askdirectory function, which displays a directory selection dialog as shown in Figure 4-10. As you can see, the baselines and alerts folders have also been created.

If the selection result is a valid directory (we use the os.path.isdir() method to verify this) then we can enable the record baseline button. In addition, if the baseline has previously been established, then the activate sensor button could also be enabled.

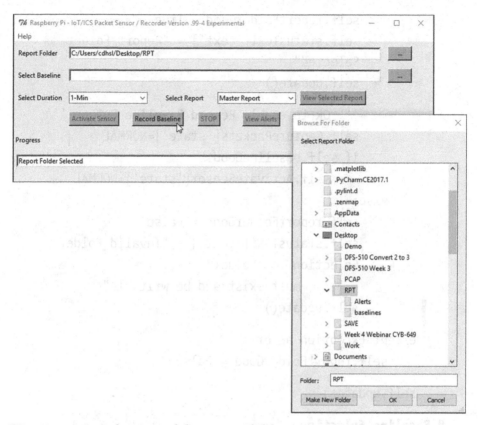

Figure 4-10. *Selection of the report folder*

Source Code Methods for GUI Elements

```
# F1 Report Folder Selection
def btnSelectFolder(self):
    try:
        self.folderSelection = tkFileDialog.
        askdirectory(initialdir="./",
                    title='Select Report Folder')

        self.ReportFolder['text'] = self.folderSelection
        if os.path.isdir(self.folderSelection) and
                    os.access(self.folderSelection, os.W_OK):
```

```
                    self.reportFolderGood = True
                    self.statusText['text'] = "Report Folder
                    Selected"
                    self.update()

                    ''' Ok to enable Record Baseline Button '''
                    self.CapturePackets['state']=NORMAL
                    if self.baselineGood:
                        self.ActivateSensor['state']=NORMAL
            else:
                    self.reportFolderGood = False
                    self.statusText['text'] = "Invalid Folder
                    Selection ... Folder
                            must exist and be writable"
                    self.update()

        except Exception as err:
            self.reportFolderGood = False

        self.update()

    # Baseline Selection
    def btnSelectBaseLine(self):
        self.fileSelection = tkFileDialog.askopenfilename(initi
        aldir="./",
                        self.fileSelection =
                        tkFileDialog.askopenfilename(initiald
                        ir="./",
                        filetypes=[("Sensor Baseline
                        Files","*.baseline")],
                        title='Select Baseline
                        File')  title='Select Baseline
                        File')

        self.fileBaseline['text'] = self.fileSelection
```

```python
    if self.fileBaseline:
    try:
        with open(self.fileSelection, 'rb') as base:
            try:
                ''' Make sure we loaded a dictionary '''
                self.baselineDictionary = pickle.
                load(base)

                ''' Make sure the elements match our
                structure'''
                if type(self.baselineDictionary) is dict:
                    value = self.baselineDictionary.
                    values()[0]
                    if value[POV] == 'S' or value[POV]
                    == 'D':
                        self.baselineGood = True
                    else:
                        self.baselineGood = False
                        self.statusText['text'] =
                        "Baseline Load Failed"

                    if self.baselineGood:
                        ''' Create Quick Lookups for
                        Country, MFG'''
                        self.statusText['text'] =
                        "Loading Baseline
                                        Contents"
                        self.update()

                        for key, value in
                                    self.
                                    baselineDictionary.
                                    iteritems():
```

97

```python
try:
    srcCC = value[SRCCC]
    dstCC = value[DSTCC]
    srcMAC = value[SRCMAC]
    dstMAC = value[DSTMAC]

    if srcCC != '' and
    srcCC.lower() !=
                'unknown':
        self.
        baselineCC[srcCC]
        = 1

    if dstCC != '' and
    dstCC.lower() !=
                'unknown':
        self.
        baselineCC[dstCC]
        = 1

    if srcMAC != '' and
    srcMAC.lower() !=
                'unknown':
        self.
        baselineMAC[srcMAC]
        = 1

    if dstMAC != '' and
    dstMAC.lower() !=
                'unknown':
        self.
        baselineMAC[dstMAC]
        = 1
except:
```

```
                              ''' ignore errors in
                          baseline

                                      loading'''
                          continue

                  self.statusText['text'] =
                  "Loading Baseline
                                    Completed"

                  ''' Ok to enable Activate
                  Sensor Button '''
                  if self.reportFolderGood:
                      self.ActivateSensor['state'
                      ]=NORMAL

          except Exception as err:
              self.statusText['text'] = "Baseline
              Load Failed"

      except Exception as err:
          self.statusText['text'] = "Baseline Load
          Failed: "+str(err)

    self.update()
```

When we examine the btnSelectBaseLine method depicted in F2, we see that this function is a bit more complicated. First, this method uses the built-in tkFileDialog.askopenfilename to select the baseline. Since the user can select any file with the .baseline extension, we need to verify that this is a valid baseline generated by the record baseline method. Once this is verified, we create a set of local dictionaries to hold extracted values from the baseline, including previously observed countries and MAC addresses; these will be used during the monitoring process to generate alerts from unknown countries and new observed MAC addresses.

Once a verified baseline and report folder have been selected, both the activate sensor and record baseline selections are available, as shown in Figure 4-11.

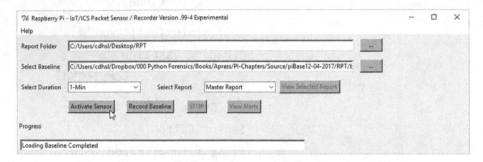

Figure 4-11. *Properly selected and verified report folder and baseline*

Record Baseline Method (btnPerformCapture)

Now we move to one of the critical methods of the application, the record baseline or btnPerformCapture method. This method utilizes two selections by the user:

- Duration (determine how long to run the recording)

- Report folder (where to record the results)

The method first performs some setup tasks (section R1) to disable the other action buttons and to enable the Stop button, allowing the user to interrupt the recording. In addition, a packet processor object is instantiated, which in turn loads the necessary lookups for manufacturer OUI identification, port and protocol translations, and country lookups. If the PaPirus display is detected and available, it will be initialized to display details of the ongoing recording.

Finally, the network adapter is set to promiscuous mode to collect all traffic presented at Eth0.

Moving to section R2, the main loop is established and processes each packet observed over the network. The loop continues until either the duration time expires or the user presses the stop button. Every 2 seconds, the packet count is updated in the status bar and the progress bar is updated marking the progress toward the time expiration.

Once R2 completes (either by the user interrupting the process or through time expiration), a new baseline is created and stored in the baseline directory, and all the HTML and CSV reports are generated and stored in the selected report folder. The code in the R3 section calls each report generation function. Let's take a deeper look at one of the report generation functions to examine how the resulting HTML reports are generated in the next section.

R1 Perform Capture

```
def btnPerformCapture(self):

    self.CapturePackets['state']=DISABLED
    saveActivateSensor = self.ActivateSensor['state']
    self.ActivateSensor['state']=DISABLED
    self.StopCapture['state']=NORMAL
    self.update()

    # create a packet processing object
    self.statusText['text'] = "Loading Lookups ..."
    self.update()

    self.packetObj = PacketProcessor(self.lookupList)

    if PA_ON:
        self.statusText['text'] = "Resetting PaPirus Display
        ... Please
            Wait"
        self.update()
        self.paObj.ResetDisplay()
```

```
        self.paObj.UpdateMode("Record ")
        self.paObj.UpdateStatus("Operation Started   ")

self.statusText['text'] = "Capturing Packets ..."
self.update()

durationValue = self.duration.get()
durSec = CONVERT[durationValue]
startTime = time.time()
curProgress = 0
self.progressBar['value'] = curProgress

# Python Packet Capture
# configure the eth0 in promiscuous mode

try:
    if platform.system() == "Linux":
        self.PLATFORM = "LINUX"

        ret =  os.system("ifconfig eth0 promisc")

        if ret == 0:
            LogEvent(LOG_INFO, 'Promiscuous Mode Enabled
            for eth0')

            # create a new socket using the python socket
            module
            # PF_PACKET     : Specifies Protocol Family
                              Packet Level
            # SOCK_RAW      : Specifies A raw network
                              packet layer
            # htons(0x0003) : Specifies all headers and
                              packets
            #                 : Ethernet and IP, including
                              TCP/UDP etc
```

```
            # attempt to open the socket for capturing raw
            packets

            rawSocket=socket.socket(socket.PF_PACKET,
                socket.SOCK_RAW,
                socket.htons(0x0003))

        else:
            self.statusText['text'] = "Capture Failed ...
            Cannot Open
                        Socket"
            self.progressBar['value'] = 0
            self.update()
            self.CapturePackets['state']=NORMAL
            self.StopCapture['state']=DISABLED
            self.update()
            return

    except Exception as err:
        self.statusText['text'] = "Network Connection Failed:
        "+ str(err)
        self.update()
        return

    pkCnt = 0
    upTime = time.time()
    paTime = time.time()

# R2 Main Loop
while True:

        curTime = time.time()
        elapsedTime = curTime - startTime

        if elapsedTime > durSec:
```

```
            break

    if self.abortFlag:

        ''' User Aborted '''
        ''' Reset the Flag for next use '''
        self.abortFlag = False
        break

    ''' Update the Progress Bar on Change vs Total Time'''
    newProgress = int(round((elapsedTime/durSec * 100)))
    if newProgress > curProgress:
        self.progressBar['value'] = newProgress
        curProgress = newProgress
        self.update()

    ''' Update the Status Window every two seconds'''
    newTime = time.time()
    if (newTime - upTime) >= 2:
        upTime = newTime
        cntStr = '{:,}'.format(pkCnt)
        self.statusText['text'] = "Connections Processed: "
        + cntStr
        self.update()

    ''' Update the PA Display if available '''
    if PA_ON:
        newPATime = time.time()
        if (newPATime - paTime) >= 20:
            paTime = newPATime
            cntStr = '{:,}'.format(pkCnt)
            self.paObj.UpdatePacketCnt(cntStr)
```

```
# attempt to receive (this call is synchronous, thus it
will wait)

try:
    recvPacket=rawSocket.recv(65535)
    self.packetObj.PacketExtractor(recvPacket)
    pkCnt += 1
except Exception as err:
    LogEvent(LOG_INFO,'Recv Packet Failed: '+str(err))
    continue

self.statusText['text'] = "Generating Capture Reports and
Saving
        Baseline ..."
self.update()

# Generate Reports and Save the Baseline
# R3 Report Generation
self.SaveOb(self.packetObj.d)
self.GenCSV(self.packetObj.d)
self.GenHTML(self.packetObj.d)
self.GenCOUNTRY(self.packetObj.d)
self.GenMFG(self.packetObj.d)
self.GenICS(self.packetObj.d)
self.GenIOT(self.packetObj.d)
self.GenPortUsage(self.packetObj.d)

''' Enable Report Button '''
self.viewReport['state']=NORMAL

''' Reset Progress Bar and Post Completed status'''
self.progressBar['value'] = 0
cntStr = '{:,}'.format(pkCnt)
```

```
unique = '{:,}'.format(len(self.packetObj.d))
    self.statusText['text'] = "Done:  Total Connections
    Processed:
            "+cntStr+"  Unique Observations Recorded: "+unique
    self.CapturePackets['state']=NORMAL

    # reset the ActivateSensor State
    self.ActivateSensor['state']=saveActivateSensor

    self.StopCapture['state']=DISABLED
    self.update()

    if PA_ON:
        self.paObj.UpdatePacketCnt(unique)
        self.paObj.UpdateStatus("Operation Completed")
        self.paObj.UpdateMode("                ")
```

Master Report Generation (GenHTML)

The report generators all work basically the same, but they filter and sort data based on the specific reports being created. The method is a unique method of autogenerating an HTML file. One could use XML (eXtensible Markup Language) and style sheets as an alternative.

Examining M1, we start by updating the status bar of our progress. The current date and time are obtained in order to generate a unique file name for the desired report. Each report name is prepended with the date-time in order to provide easy sorting of the report results. For this example, the report name would be in the following format:

```
2017-11-14-08-22-master.html
yyyy-mm-dd-hr-mm-master.html
```

Next, the html file is built from a template stored in the rpt.py file. Each report has a separate template that is used. Basically, the template contains an HTML_START section, HTML_HEADER section, (multiple) HTML_BODY sections, and HTML_END section.

Examining the code in section M2, the Python dictionary object *d* contains all the unique observations collected during this recording. A loop is created to iterate over each unique observation, and the values extracted from the key/value pairs of the dictionary are stored in local variable prefaced with *fld* (for example, *fldAlert, fldSrcIP,* etc.). Once they are collected we use the format method available for strings, as shown here, to replace the placeholders defined in the template HTML.

```
htmlSection = htmlSection.format(**locals())
```

The template HTML placeholders highlighted here are then replaced by the corresponding local variables to generate the final HTML code.

```
<td style="width: 250px;"> {fldAlert} </td>
<td style="width: 250px;"> {fldAlertCnt} </td>
```

Once all the HTML code has been generated, the code in section M3 writes out the complete *htmlContents* to the report filename created in section M1.

```
def GenHTML(self, d):
# M1 Update Report Date / Time
    ''' Produce the Master Report using the master dictionary
    provided '''

    path = self.ReportFolder['text']

    utc=datetime.datetime.utcnow()
    yr = str(utc.year)
    mt = '{:02d}'.format(utc.month)
    dy = '{:02d}'.format(utc.day)
```

```
hr = '{:02d}'.format(utc.hour)
mn = '{:02d}'.format(utc.minute)

''' Produce Master HTML Report'''
self.statusText['text'] = "Generating Master HTML Report
..."+yr+'-
    '+mt+'-'+dy+'-'+hr+'-'+mn+"
    -Master.html"

self.update()

filename = yr+'-'+mt+'-'+dy+'-'+hr+'-'+mn+"-Master.hmtl"
self.MasterHTML = os.path.join(path, filename)

htmlContents = ''
htmlHeader = rpt.HTML_START

fldDate = yr+'-'+mt+'-'+dy+'@'+hr+':'+mn+" UTC"
htmlHeader = htmlHeader.format(**locals())
htmlContents = htmlContents + htmlHeader

for eachKey in d:
# M2 Adding Observation Data to the Reports
    htmlSection = rpt.HTML_BODY
    value = d[eachKey]
    fldAlert      = value[ALERT]
    fldSrcIP      = eachKey[SRCIP]
    fldDstIP      = eachKey[DSTIP]
    fldFrame      = eachKey[FRAMETYPE]
    fldProtocol   = eachKey[PROTOCOL]

    fldSrcPort    = value[SRCPORT]
    fldSrcPortName= value[SRCPORTNAME]
    fldDstPort    = value[DSTPORT]
```

```
fldDstPortName= value[DSTPORTNAME]
fldSrcMAC      = value[SRCMAC]
fldDstMAC      = value[DSTMAC]
fldSrcMFG      = value[SRCMFG]
fldDstMFG      = value[DSTMFG]
fldSrcCC       = value[SRCCC]
fldDstCC       = value[DSTCC]
fldPktSize     = value[AVGPCKSIZE]
fldTwilight    = value[AM12]
fldMorning     = value[AM6]
fldAfternoon   = value[PM12]
fldEvening     = value[PM6]
fldWeekend     = value[WKEND]
fldTotal       = value[AM12]+value[AM6]+
                        value[PM12]+
                        value[PM6]+value[WKEND]

    htmlSection = htmlSection.format(**locals())
    htmlContents = htmlContents + htmlSection

htmlContents = htmlContents + rpt.HTML_END


''' Write the Report to the output file'''
# M3 Write HTML Report to File
output = open(self.MasterHTML,"w")
output.write(htmlContents)
output.close()
```

Saving the Baseline (SaveOb)

In addition to generating the various reports associated with the
record baseline process, the actual baseline is also created. This is a
straightforward process in Python, as we are serializing the Python
dictionary object *d* using the pickle standard library module.

Note   What is pickling? Pickling "serializes" Python objects prior
to writing them to a file. Pickling converts Python objects (list, dict,
etc.) into a character stream. The idea is that this character stream
contains all the information necessary to reconstruct the object in
another Python script. This is done by using the pickle.load(filename)
method. This method was utilized in section F-2 when the baseline
file was selected by the user.

In Section S1, the SaveOb method uses the same naming convention
used when creating report files, but adds the file extension ".baseline" to
the file. Then with only two lines of code, the baseline file is created.

```
with open(outFile, 'wb') as fp:
    pickle.dump(d, fp)
```

```
def SaveOb(self, d):
# S1 Serializing and Saving the Object Baseline
    ''' Save the current observation dictionary to a the
    specified path '''
    try:
        path = self.ReportFolder['text']
        baseDir = os.path.join(path,'baselines')
        if not os.path.isdir(baseDir):
            os.mkdir(baseDir)

        self.statusText['text'] = "Generating Serialized
        Baseline ..."
        self.update()

        utc=datetime.datetime.utcnow()
        yr = str(utc.year)
        mt = '{:02d}'.format(utc.month)
        dy = '{:02d}'.format(utc.day)
```

```
    hr = '{:02d}'.format(utc.hour)
    mn = '{:02d}'.format(utc.minute)

    filename = yr+'-'+mt+'-'+dy+'--'+hr+'-'+mn+".baseline"
    outFile = os.path.join(baseDir, filename)
    with open(outFile, 'wb') as fp:
        pickle.dump(d, fp)

except Exception as err:
    LogEvent(LOG_ERR, "Failed to Create Baseline
    Output"+str(err))
```

Activate Sensor (btnActivateSensor, PacketMonitor)

The final method to examine in this chapter is the btnActivateSensor method. The front end of this method mimics that of the packer recorder. The difference is in the processing of each received packet. The PacketMonitor method examines the received packet and determines if "the same packet construction" exists in the current baseline. If not, then an alert report item is generated to indicate a "New Observation". In addition, the key elements of the packet, such as IP country location, MAC address, packet size, and time of the observation, are compared to known or expected values. If anomalies are discovered, additional report items are recorded. The following code snippet includes the *btnActivateSensor*, *PacketMonitor*, and supporting methods.

```
def btnActivateSensor(self):
    # Handle Active Sensor Button Click

    self.ActivateSensor['state']=DISABLED
    saveCaptureState = self.CapturePackets['state']
    self.CapturePackets['state']=DISABLED
    self.StopCapture['state']=NORMAL
    self.update()
```

```python
    # create a packet processing object
    self.statusText['text'] = "Loading Lookups ..."
    self.update()

    self.packetObj = PacketProcessor(self.lookupList,
            self.baselineDictionary)
  self.statusText['text'] = "Monitoring Packets ..."
  if PA_ON:
      self.statusText['text'] = "Resetting PaPirus Display
      ... Please
          Wait"
      self.update()
      self.paObj.ResetDisplay()
      self.paObj.UpdateMode("Monitor")
      self.paObj.UpdateStatus("Operation Started  ")

  self.statusText['text'] = "Monitoring Packets ..."
  self.update()

  durationValue = self.duration.get()
  durSec = CONVERT[durationValue]
  startTime = time.time()
  curProgress = 0
  self.progressBar['value'] = curProgress

  self.alertDict = {}


  # Python Packet Capture
  # configure the eth0 in promiscuous mode

  try:
      ret =  os.system("ifconfig eth0 promisc")

      if ret == 0:
```

```
    LogEvent(LOG_INFO, 'Promiscuous Mode Enabled for
    eth0')

    # create a new socket using the python socket
    module
    # PF_PACKET     : Specifies Protocol Family Packet
                      Level
    # SOCK_RAW      : Specifies A raw protocol at the
                      network layer
    # htons(0x0003) : Specifies all headers and packets
    #               : Ethernet and IP, including TCP/
                      UDP etc

    # attempt to open the socket for capturing raw
    packets

    rawSocket=socket.socket(socket.PF_PACKET,socket.
    SOCK_RAW,
        socket.htons(0x0003))
else:
    self.statusText['text'] = "Monitoring Failed ...
        Cannot Open Socket"
    self.progressBar['value'] = 0
    self.update()
    self.CapturePackets['state']=NORMAL
    self.StopCapture['state']=DISABLED
    self.update()
    return

except Exception as err:
    self.statusText['text'] = "Socket Exception ...
    "+str(err)
    self.progressBar['value'] = 0
```

```python
        self.CapturePackets['state']=NORMAL
        self.StopCapture['state']=DISABLED
        self.update()

        return

    pkCnt = 0
    upTime = time.time()
    paTime = time.time()

    while True:

        curTime = time.time()
        elapsedTime = curTime - startTime

        if elapsedTime > durSec:
            break

        if self.abortFlag:

            ''' User Aborted '''
            ''' Reset the Flag for next use '''
            self.abortFlag = False
            break

        ''' Update the Progress Bar on Change vs Total Time'''
        newProgress = int(round((elapsedTime/durSec * 100)))
        if newProgress > curProgress:
            self.progressBar['value'] = newProgress
            curProgress = newProgress
            self.update()

        ''' Update the Status Window every two seconds'''
        newTime = time.time()
        if (newTime - upTime) >= 2:
            upTime = newTime
```

```
        cntStr = '{:,}'.format(pkCnt)
        self.statusText['text'] = "Pck Cnt: " + cntStr
        self.update()

    ''' Update the PA Display if available '''
    if PA_ON:
        newPATime = time.time()
        if (newPATime - paTime) >= 20:
            paTime = newPATime
            cntStr = '{:,}'.format(pkCnt)
            self.paObj.UpdatePacketCnt(cntStr)

    # attempt to receive (this call is synchronous, thus it
    will wait)

    try:
        recvPacket=rawSocket.recv(65535)
        self.packetObj.PacketMonitor(recvPacket,
            self.alertDict, self.baselineCC,
            self.baselineMAC)
        pkCnt += 1
    except Exception as err:
        LogEvent(LOG_INFO,'Recv Packet Failed: '+str(err))
        continue

# Generate Sensor Reports

self.GenAlerts(self.alertDict)

''' Enable Report Button '''
self.ViewAlerts['state']=NORMAL

''' Reset Progress Bar and Post Completed status'''
self.progressBar['value'] = 0
cntStr = '{:,}'.format(pkCnt)
```

```
alertsGenerated = '{:,}'.format(len(self.alertDict))
self.statusText['text'] = "Done:  Total Connections
Processed
    :  "+cntStr+"  Alerts: "+alertsGenerated

self.CapturePackets['state'] = saveCaptureState
self.ActivateSensor['state']=NORMAL
self.StopCapture['state']=DISABLED
self.update()

if PA_ON:
    self.paObj.UpdateAlertCnt(alertsGenerated)
    self.paObj.UpdatePacketCnt(cntStr)
    self.paObj.UpdateStatus("Operation Completed")
    self.paObj.UpdateMode("              ")
```

def *PacketMonitor* (self, packet, alertDict, baseCC, baseMAC):

```
''' Extract Packet Data input: string packet, dictionary d
    result is to update dictionary d
'''

ETH_LEN  = 14       # ETHERNET HDR LENGTH
IP_LEN   = 20       # IP HEADER     LENGTH
IPv6_LEN = 40       # IPv6 HEADER   LENGTH
ARP_HDR  = 8        # ARP HEADER
UDP_LEN  = 8        # UPD HEADER    LENGTH
TCP_LEN  = 20       # TCP HEADER    LENGTH

''' Elements of the key '''

self.srcMac = ''
self.dstMac = ''
self.frType = ''
self.srcIP  = ''
```

```
self.dstIP  = ''
self.proto  = ''
self.opcode = ''
self.port   = ''
self.srcPort = ''
self.dstPort = ''
self.srcPortName = ''
self.dstPortName = ''
self.packetSize = 0
self.srcMFG = ''
self.dstMFG = ''
self.dstMacOui =''
self.srcMacOui = ''
self.srcCC = ''
self.dstCC = ''
self.alert = ''

self.lastObservationTime = time.ctime(time.time())

ethernetHeader=packet[0:ETH_LEN]
ethFields =struct.unpack("!6s6sH",ethernetHeader)

self.dstMac = hexlify(ethFields[0]).upper()
self.dstMacOui = self.dstMac[0:6]
self.dstMFG = self.ouiOBJ.lookup(self.dstMacOui)
self.alert = 'Normal'

self.srcMac    = hexlify(ethFields[1]).upper()
self.srcMacOui = self.srcMac[0:6]
self.srcMFG    = self.ouiOBJ.lookup(self.srcMacOui)

self.fType  = ethFields[2]

frameType = self.ethOBJ.lookup(self.fType)
self.frType = frameType
```

```
if frameType == "IPV4":
    # Process as IPv4 Packet
    ipHeader = packet[ETH_LEN:ETH_LEN+IP_LEN]

    # unpack the ip header fields
    ipHeaderTuple = struct.unpack('!BBHHHBBH4s4s' , ipHeader)

    # extract the key ip header fields of interest
                                        # Field Contents
    verLen        = ipHeaderTuple[0]    # Field 0: Version &
                                          Length
    TOS           = ipHeaderTuple[1]    # Field 1: Type of
                                          Service
    packetLength = ipHeaderTuple[2]     # Field 2: Packet
                                          Length
    protocol      = ipHeaderTuple[6]    # Field 6: Protocol
                                          Number
    sourceIP      = ipHeaderTuple[8]    # Field 8: Source IP
    destIP        = ipHeaderTuple[9]    # Field 9:
                                          Destination IP
    timeToLive    = ipHeaderTuple[5]    # Field 5: Time to
                                          Live

    # Calculate / Convert extracted values

    version       = verLen >> 4    # Upper Nibble is the
                                     version Number
    length        = verLen & 0x0F  # Lower Nibble represents
                                     the size
    ipHdrLength   = length * 4     # Calculate the header size
                                     in bytes

    # covert the srcIP/dstIP to typical dotted notation strings

    self.packetSize = packetLength
```

```
self.srcIP = socket.inet_ntoa(sourceIP);
self.dstIP = socket.inet_ntoa(destIP);

self.srcCC = self.cc.lookup(self.srcIP, 'IPv4')
self.dstCC = self.cc.lookup(self.dstIP, 'IPv4')

translate = self.traOBJ.lookup(str(protocol))
transProtocol = translate[0]

if transProtocol == 'TCP':

    self.proto = "TCP"

    stripTCPHeader = packet[ETH_
    LEN+ipHdrLength:ipHdrLength+
                        ETH_LEN+TCP_LEN]

    # unpack the TCP Header to obtain the
    # source and destination port

    tcpHeaderBuffer = struct.unpack('!HHLLBBHHH' ,
    stripTCPHeader)

    self.srcPort = tcpHeaderBuffer[0]
    self.dstPort = tcpHeaderBuffer[1]

    self.srcPortName = self.portOBJ.lookup(self.srcPort,
    'TCP')
    self.dstPortName = self.portOBJ.lookup(self.dstPort,
    'TCP')

elif transProtocol == 'UDP':

    self.proto = "UDP"

    stripUDPHeader = packet[ETH_LEN+ipHdrLength:ETH_LEN+
                        ipHdrLength+UDP_LEN]
```

```
        # unpack the UDP packet and obtain the
        # source and destination port

        udpHeaderBuffer = struct.unpack('!HHHH' ,
        stripUDPHeader)

        self.srcPort = udpHeaderBuffer[0]
        self.dstPort = udpHeaderBuffer[1]

        self.srcPortName = self.portOBJ.lookup(self.srcPort,
        'UDP')
        self.dstPortName = self.portOBJ.lookup(self.dstPort,
        'UDP')

    elif transProtocol == 'ICMP':

        self.proto = "ICMP"

    elif transProtocol == 'IGMP':

        self.proto = "IGMP"

    else:
        self.proto = transProtocol

elif frameType == 'ARP':

    # Process as IPv4 Packet
    arpHeader = packet[ETH_LEN:ETH_LEN+ARP_HDR]

    # unpack the ARP header fields
    arpHeaderTuple = struct.unpack('!HHBBH' , arpHeader)

    ht = arpHeaderTuple[0]
    pt = arpHeaderTuple[1]
    hal = arpHeaderTuple[2]
```

```
    pal = arpHeaderTuple[3]
    op  = arpHeaderTuple[4]

    # set packetSize for ARP to zero
    self.packetSize = 0

    base = ETH_LEN+ARP_HDR

    shAddr = hexlify(packet[base:base+hal])
    base = base+hal
    spAddr = hexlify(packet[base:base+pal])
    base = base+pal
    thAddr = hexlify(packet[base:base+hal])
    base = base+hal
    tpAddr = hexlify(packet[base:base+pal])

    self.srcIP = shAddr
    self.dstIP = thAddr
    self.proto = str(op)

elif frameType == "IPV6":

    # Process as IPv6 Packet
    ipHeader = packet[ETH_LEN:ETH_LEN+IPv6_LEN]

    # unpack the ip header fields
    ipv6HeaderTuple = struct.unpack('!IHBBQQQQ' , ipHeader)

    flush = ipv6HeaderTuple[0]
    pLength = ipv6HeaderTuple[1]
    nextHdr = ipv6HeaderTuple[2]
    hopLmt  = ipv6HeaderTuple[3]
    srcIP   = (ipv6HeaderTuple[4] << 64) | ipv6HeaderTuple[5]
    dstIP   = (ipv6HeaderTuple[6] << 64) | ipv6HeaderTuple[7]

    self.packetSize = pLength
    self.srcIP = str(netaddr.IPAddress(srcIP))
```

```python
        self.dstIP = str(netaddr.IPAddress(dstIP))

        self.srcCC = self.cc.lookup(self.srcIP, 'IPv6')
        self.dstCC = self.cc.lookup(self.dstIP, 'IPv6')

        translate = self.traOBJ.lookup(str(nextHdr))
        transProtocol = translate[0]

        if transProtocol == 'TCP':

            self.proto = "TCP"

            stripTCPHeader = packet[ETH_LEN+IPv6_LEN:ETH_LEN+
                                IPv6_LEN+TCP_LEN]

            # unpack the TCP Header to obtain the
            # source and destination port

            tcpHeaderBuffer = struct.unpack('!HHLLBBHHH' ,
            stripTCPHeader)

            self.srcPort = tcpHeaderBuffer[0]
            self.dstPort = tcpHeaderBuffer[1]

            self.srcPortName = self.portOBJ.lookup(self.srcPort,
            'TCP')
            self.dstPortName = self.portOBJ.lookup(self.dstPort,
            'TCP')

        elif transProtocol == 'UDP':

            self.proto = "UDP"

            stripUDPHeader = packet[ETH_LEN+IPv6_LEN:ETH_LEN+
                                IPv6_LEN+UDP_LEN]

            # unpack the UDP packet and obtain the
            # source and destination port
```

```
        udpHeaderBuffer = struct.unpack('!HHHH' ,
        stripUDPHeader)

        self.srcPort = udpHeaderBuffer[0]
        self.dstPort = udpHeaderBuffer[1]

        self.srcPortName = self.portOBJ.lookup(self.srcPort,
        'UDP')
        self.dstPortName = self.portOBJ.lookup(self.dstPort,
        'UDP')

    elif transProtocol == 'ICMP':

        self.proto = "ICMP"

    elif transProtocol == 'IGMP':

        self.proto = "IGMP"
    else:
        self.proto = transProtocol

else:
    self.proto = frameType

valueNdx = getOccurrenceValue()

if self.srcIP == '127.0.0.1' and self.dstIP == '127.0.0.1':
    ''' Ignore this packet '''
    return

if self.srcPort <= CORE_PORTS:
    ''' if srcPort is definately a service port'''
    key = (self.srcIP, self.dstIP, self.srcPort,
            self.frType, self.proto)

elif self.dstPort <= CORE_PORTS:
```

```python
        ''' if dstPort is definately a service port'''
        key = (self.srcIP, self.dstIP, self.dstPort,
               self.frType, self.proto)

elif self.srcPort < self.dstPort:
        ''' Guess that srcPort is server '''
        key = (self.srcIP, self.dstIP, self.srcPort,
               self.frType, self.proto)
else:
        ''' guess destination port is server'''
        key = (self.srcIP, self.dstIP, self.dstPort,
               self.frType, self.proto)

''' Check Baseline for previously observed key '''

try:
        ''' if match found, snag the time entries and avg packet
        size'''
        value = self.b[key]
        avgPckSize = value[AVGPCKSIZE]
        timeList = [value[AM12], value[AM6], value[PM12],
                    value[PM6], value[WKEND]]
        newEntry = False
except:
        ''' Then this is a new observation'''
        self.CreateAlertEntry(key, alertDict, "New Observation")
        newEntry = True

chk, value = self.ouiOBJ.chkHotlist(self.dstMacOui)
if chk:
        self.CreateAlertEntry(key, alertDict, "HotList: "+value)

if self.isNewMAC(self.srcMac, baseMAC):
        self.CreateAlertEntry(key, alertDict, "New MAC Address")
```

124

```
if self.isNewMAC(self.dstMac, baseMAC):
    self.CreateAlertEntry(key, alertDict, "New MAC Address")

if self.isNewCC(self.srcCC, baseCC):
    self.CreateAlertEntry(key, alertDict, "New Country Code")

if self.isNewCC(self.dstCC, baseCC):
    self.CreateAlertEntry(key, alertDict, "New Country Code")

''' If this is not a new entry the safe to check pckSize and
Times'''
if not newEntry:
    if self.isUnusualPckSize(self.packetSize, avgPckSize):
        self.CreateAlertEntry(key, alertDict, "Unusual Packet
        Size")

    if self.isUnusualTime(timeList):
        self.CreateAlertEntry(key, alertDict, "Unusual Packet
        Time")
```

Packet Monitor Supporting Methods

```
def isUnusualPckSize(self, pSize, avgSize):
        if float(pSize) < float(avgSize*.70):
            return True
        if float(pSize) < float(avgSize*1.30):
            return True
        return False

    def isNewMAC(self, mac, b):
        if mac == 'Unknown' or mac == '':
            return False
        if not mac in b:
            return True
        else:
```

```
            return False

    def isNewCC(self,cc, b):
        if cc == 'Unknown' or cc == '':
            return False
        if not cc in b:
            return True
        else:
            return False

    def isUnusualTime(self, occList):

        occ = getOccurrenceValue()
        if occList[occ] == 0:
            return True
        else:
            return False

    def CreateAlertEntry(self, key, alertDict, alertType):
        try:
            ''' See if the alert already exists '''
            value = alertDict[key]
            ''' if yes, then bump the occurrence count'''
            cnt = value[1] + 1
            alertDict[key] = [alertType, cnt,
                              self.lastObservationTime,
                              self.packetSize,
                              self.srcCC, self.dstCC, self.
                              srcMac,
                              self.dstMac, self.srcMFG, self.
                              dstMFG,
                              self.srcPort, self.dstPort, self.
                              srcPortName,
```

```
                          self.dstPortName ]
    except:
        ''' Othewise create a new alert entry'''
        alertDict[key] = [alertType, 1, self.
        lastObservationTime,
                          self.packetSize, self.srcCC,
                          self.dstCC,
                          self.srcMac, self.dstMac, self.
                          srcMFG,
                          self.dstMFG,self.srcPort, self.
                          dstPort,
                          self.srcPortName, self.
                          dstPortName ]
```

Summary

This chapter provided both an overview of the Raspberry Pi sensor/ recorder along with a detailed examination of many of the code elements that support the design. This included the following:

- Design overview

- Examination of the GUI approach

- Integration of the PaPirus ePaper display

- Details of the baseline recording method

- Details of the sensor methods

- Details of the report generation methods

- Finally, the use of the Python pickle method to store and load the resulting recorded baselines

In Chapter 5, the focus will be on applying the Pi recorder/sensor to create baselines that are used to train and then activate the sensor. Finally, both the recorder-generated reports and the reports generated by the sensor will be examined to expose IoT-based operations within our test network.

CHAPTER 5

Operating the Raspberry Pi Sensor

Now that we have a functioning Raspberry Pi sensor that includes the baseline recorder, sensor, and reports, let's do an operational walk-through.

Raspberry Pi Setup

The first step is to set up the Raspberry Pi sensor.

The following is required for the basic installation:

1. Raspberry Pi Model 3

2. Minimum of 16GB SD card

3. Install the Raspbian OS (this is the current version running)

   ```
   PRETTY_NAME="Raspbian GNU/Linux 8 (jessie)"
   NAME="Raspbian GNU/Linux"
   VERSION_ID="8"
   VERSION="8 (jessie)"
   ID=raspbian
   ID_LIKE=debian
   ```

© Chet Hosmer 2018
C. Hosmer, *Defending IoT Infrastructures with the Raspberry Pi*,
https://doi.org/10.1007/978-1-4842-3700-7_5

4. Once you have this installed, update the Python
    2.7 version to the latest, which currently is 2.7.9 or
    greater. Note this step is only necessary if you plan
    to work with the Python source code. The executable
    for piSensorV3 is also being provided with this book.

5. Copy installation files available at python-forensics.
    org/piSensor to a folder of your choice on the Pi.
    For my test installation, I placed the files in a folder
    named TEST right on the desktop of the Pi. Figure 5-1
    depicts the contents of the folder TEST.

    a. RPT Folder: Reports and baselines are written to
        this folder by the Raspberry Pi sensor

    b. piSensorV3 is the compiled Python sensor
        application

    c. lookup.db contains the various lookup tables for
        ports, protocols, MAC address manufacturers,
        and Ethernet types

    d. The geoIPv6 and geoIPv4 files are used to map
        IP addresses to country locations

    e. hotlist.txt contains a list of ports of interest

File Edit View Bookmarks Go Tools Help				
/home/pi/Desktop/TEST				
Directory Tree	Name	Description	Size	Modified
⊟ 🖿 pi	📁 RPT	folder		12/18/2017 12:10
⊞ ☐ Adafruit_Python_CharLCD	📄 piSensorV3	executable	9.8 MiB	12/04/2017 13:41
⊟ 🖼 Desktop	📄 lookup.db	plain text document	2.8 MiB	11/30/2017 06:54
⊞ ☐ save	📄 hotlist.txt	plain text document	449 bytes	10/25/2017 08:04
⊞ ☐ ss	📄 geoIPv6.dat	unknown	2.0 MiB	10/04/2017 11:18
◻ 🖿 TEST	📄 geoIPv4.dat	unknown	1.1 MiB	10/04/2017 11:17

Figure 5-1. *Operational folder*

Optional Features:

As discussed in Chapter 4, you can add the PaPirus ePaper display to your Pi, as shown in Figure 5-2. This will display real-time information directly on the Pi. If the PaPirus is not installed, the sensor will perform normally and all display will be provided via the GUI only.

Figure 5-2. *Raspberry Pi with PaPirus ePaper display*

Connecting the Raspberry Pi

The next step is to connect the Raspberry Pi to the network you wish to monitor.

Switch Configuration for Packet Capture

Most modern networking infrastructures and switches support port mirroring via a Switched Port ANalyzer (SPAN) or Remote Switched Port ANalyzer (RSPAN). I'm using a TP-LINK eight-port Gigabit Easy Smart Switch TL-SG108E as shown in Figure 5-3. I have experimented with many switches and hubs for this purpose, and for a low-cost, reliable, and easy-to-configure device, this meets all my objectives.

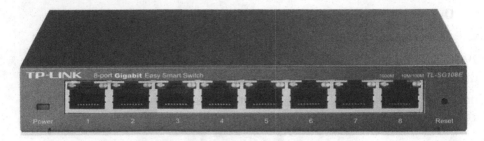

Figure 5-3. *TP-LINK eight-port Gigabit Easy Smart Switch*

The simplicity of the switch is based on the software application "Easy Smart Configuration Utility," shown in Figure 5-4, that is included with the switch. The configuration utility allows for the configuration of all the features available on the TL-SG108E.

For the purposes of capturing all the network traffic that passes through the switch, we will set up the monitoring selection. Figure 5-4 depicts the configuration screen for port monitoring. In this example, I have set up Port 8 to be the monitoring port and ports 1–7 to be monitored. This means that all traffic flowing in or out of ports 1–7 will be available for monitoring on Port 8.

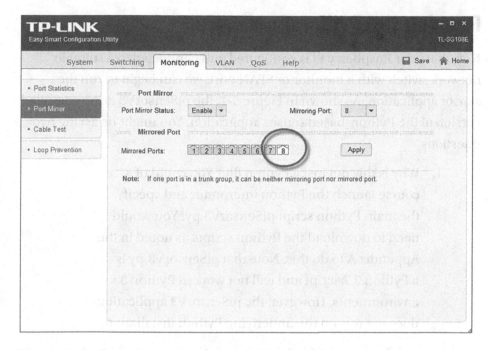

Figure 5-4. *Easy Smart configuration utility*

Now simply connect the Ethernet port on the Raspberry Pi to Port 8 on the switch as shown in Figure 5-5.

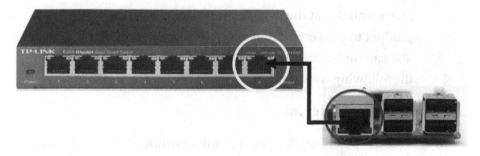

Figure 5-5. *Connecting the Pi sensor to the TP-LINK monitoring port*

Running the Python Application

Now that your Raspberry Pi is configured and connected to a suitable network switch with a monitor or SPAN port, we can begin to run the sensor application. As shown in Figure 5-1, the piSensorV3 is the compiled version of the Python-based sensor application. You might be asking two questions.

1. Why is this not just a Python file? You could of course launch the Python interpreter and specify the main Python script piSensorV3.py. You would need to download the Python scripts as noted in the Appendix A to do this. Note that piSensorV3.py is a Python 2.7 script and will not work in Python 3.x environments. However, the piSensorV3 application does not rely on the underlying Python installation.

    ```
    sudo python piSensorV3.py
    ```

2. How did you make the Python script into an executable? There are several methods to convert Python scripts into more traditional executables. I have found that the pyinstaller is an outstanding product to convert Python scripts into executables. You can find more information about pyinstaller at the following website:

    ```
    www.pyinstaller.org/
    ```

To execute the piSensorV3, open a terminal window on your Raspberry Pi. The straightforward way to do this is to click the icon on the top toolbar as shown in Figure 5-6.

Figure 5-6. *Open a terminal window*

This will launch the terminal application allowing you to type command-line commands (see Figure 5-7). To launch piSensorV3, simply

1. Navigate to the folder where you copied the required files. On my Raspberry Pi, I navigated to the desktop, then to the TEST folder. I then typed "ls" to verify that the directory contained the required files.

2. Launch the executable. Notice that I launched the executable from the current working directory, and I launched this as sudo. This is required since piSensorV3 requires privilege to place the network adapter in promiscuous mode.

```
File  Edit  Tabs  Help
pi@raspberrypi:~ $ cd Desktop
pi@raspberrypi:~/Desktop $ cd TEST
pi@raspberrypi:~/Desktop/TEST $ ls
geoIPv4.dat   hotlist.txt   lookup.db    RPT
geoIPv6.dat   log.txt       piSensorV3
pi@raspberrypi:~/Desktop/TEST $ sudo ./piSensorV3
```

Figure 5-7. *Terminal window execution of piSensorV3*

This will launch the piSensorV3 application with a GUI as shown in Figure 5-8.

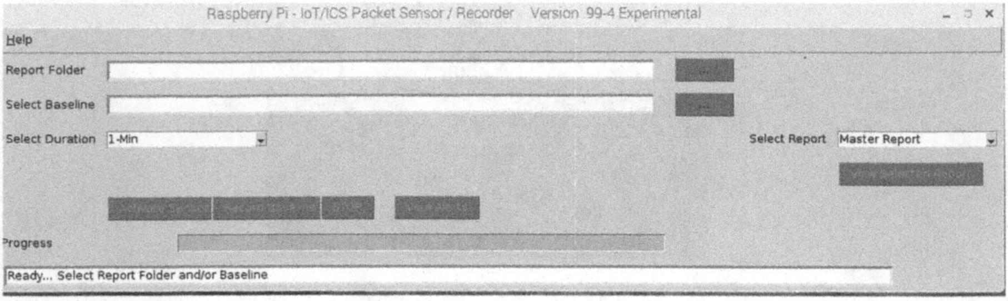

Figure 5-8. *piSensorV3 application launched*

Note   If you have a PaPirus display installed, the display will be initialized and display the initial prompts.

Creating a Baseline

The next step in the operation is to create a baseline of the network you are monitoring. This will be used by the sensor later to monitor device behaviors when in sensor mode. However, much can be gleaned about your network by recording the baseline as well.

The first step in creating the baseline is to specify the folder where the observed results will be recorded along with a setup of reports. For this I have selected the folder RPT to store the results, as shown in Figures 5-9 and 5-10. I have also selected a duration of 1 day. The duration for recording is dependent upon the behavior you wish to monitor. In most cases, I like to set this for one full week to cover operations of each day of the week.

Figure 5-9. *Report folder selection*

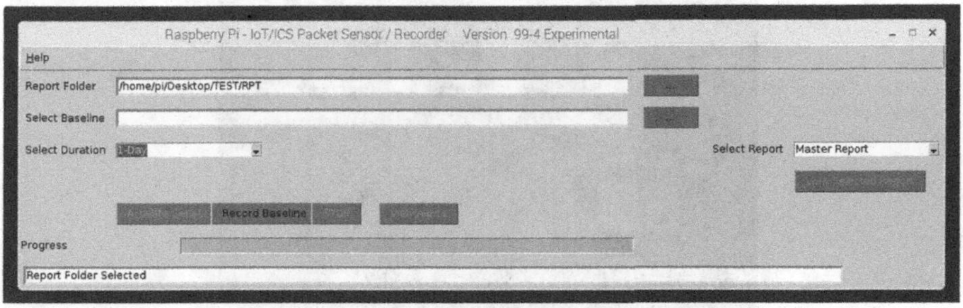

Figure 5-10. *Report and duration selected*

You may notice that the record baseline button is now available, as I have successfully specified the report folder and duration. Now that I'm ready to record the baseline, I can do that by clicking the record baseline button. Figure 5-11 shows the record baseline progress, while Figure 5-12 depicts the PaPirus display progress indications. Notice that the record baseline button is no longer available, but the STOP button is. At any time you can press STOP and you will be given the option to continue the recording or cancel it. If you cancel, the results recorded will be saved in a baseline and the resulting intermediate reports will be generated.

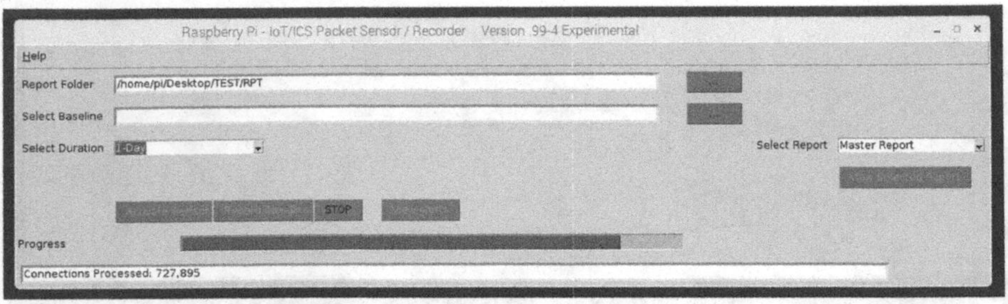

Figure 5-11. *Baseline recording progress*

Figure 5-12. *PaPirus recording progress display*

Once the recording has completed, the status message changes to "Completed" and displays the total connections processed along with the number of unique observations (see Figures 5-13 and 5-14). This is a key of our data reduction methodology. Connections using the same source IP, destination, and port are recorded. However, instead of keeping each connection, the number of connections of this type that occur are recorded for each day of the week and hour of the day. This information is used by the sensor to identify unusual behavior. This allows us to also conserve resources on the Pi by only recording unique behaviors.

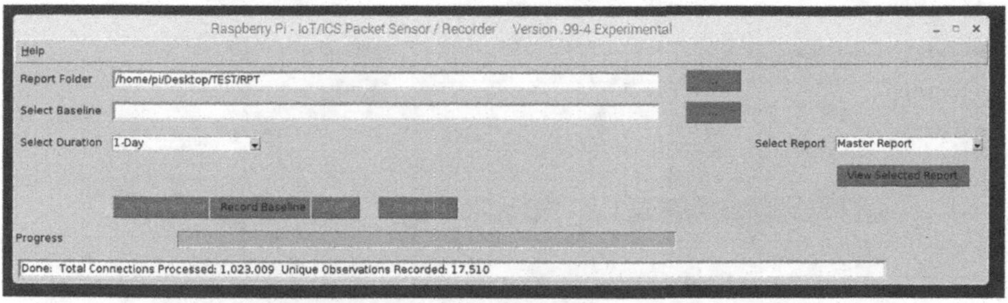

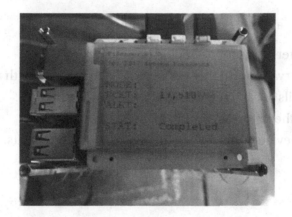

Figure 5-13. *Baseline recording completed*

Figure 5-14. *Baseline completed PaPirus display*

There are a couple of other important results of the recording operation. First, the view reports button is now activated as reports from the observation period have been generated. Figure 5-15 depicts the selection of reports that are available.

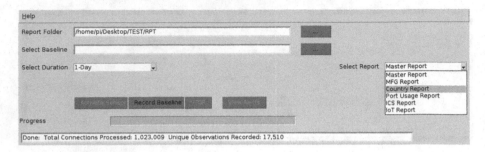

Figure 5-15. *Report selection*

The reports available include the following:

1. Master - This report includes all recorded
    observations (in this example, 17,510 records) with
    details of each recording as shown in Figure 5-15.
    See the report excerpt in Figure 5-16 for an
    abbreviated example of the master report contents.

Master Report 2017-12-30@20:00 UTC

Observations

Alert	Normal		
Src-IP	Dst-IP	Protocol	Frame-Type
192.168.86.36	192.168.86.1	UDP	IPV4
Src-Port	Src-Port Name	Dst-Port	Dst-Port name
60465	Unknown	53	Domain Name Server
Src-MAC	Src-MFG Name	Dst-MAC	Dst-MFG Name
14B31F07219E	US: Dell Inc.	E4F042BF5185	Unknown
Src Country	Dst Country		
Internal	Internal		
Packet-Size	77		
Morning	0		
Afternoon	2		
Evening	0		
PreDawn	0		
Weekend	0		
Total	2		

Alert	Normal		
Src-IP	Dst-IP	Protocol	Frame-Type
192.168.86.44	239.255.255.250	UDP	IPV4
Src-Port	Src-Port Name	Dst-Port	Dst-Port name
44868	Unknown	1900	UPnP SSDP
Src-MAC	Src-MFG Name	Dst-MAC	Dst-MFG Name
000C8A979D36	US: Bose Corporation	01005E7FFFFA	Unknown
Src Country	Dst Country		
Internal	Unknown		
Packet-Size	0		
Morning	1432		
Afternoon	1440		
Evening	1437		
PreDawn	1440		
Weekend	0		
Total	5749		

Figure 5-16. *Master report excerpt*

Master Report 2017-12-30@20:00 UTC

Observations

Alert	Normal		
Src-IP	Dst-IP	Protocol	Frame-Type
192.168.86.36	192.168.86.1	UDP	IPV4
Src-Port	Src-Port Name	Dst-Port	Dst-Port name
60465	Unknown	53	Domain Name Server
Src-MAC	Src-MFG Name	Dst-MAC	Dst-MFG Name
14B31F07219E	US: Dell Inc.	E4F042BF5185	Unknown
Src Country	Dst Country		
Internal	Internal		
Packet-Size	77		
Morning	0		
Afternoon	2		
Evening	0		
PreDawn	0		
Weekend	0		
Total	2		

Alert	Normal		
Src-IP	Dst-IP	Protocol	Frame-Type
192.168.86.44	239.255.255.250	UDP	IPV4
Src-Port	Src-Port Name	Dst-Port	Dst-Port name
44868	Unknown	1900	UPnP SSDP
Src-MAC	Src-MFG Name	Dst-MAC	Dst-MFG Name
000C8A979D36	US: Bose Corporation	01005E7FFFFA	Unknown
Src Country	Dst Country		
Internal	Unknown		
Packet-Size	0		
Morning	1432		
Afternoon	1440		
Evening	1437		
PreDawn	1440		
Weekend	0		
Total	5749		

Figure 5-17. *Master report excerpt continued*

2. Device manufacturer report – This report provides
    observation of each device manufacturer along with
    the associated MAC and IP address. This provides
    detailed tracking of known and possibly unknown
    devices located on your network. During the sensor
    phase, any device that was not observed during
    the recording period is reported as an alert. See the
    report in Figure 5-18 for an abbreviated example.

Manufacturer Report 2017-12-30@20:19 UTC

MFG Observations

Manufacturer	MAC Address	IP Address
CN: B-Link Electronic Limited	48022A4A2DAE	192.168.86.41
CN: B-Link Electronic Limited	48022A4A2DAE	48022a4a2dae
CN: B-Link Electronic Limited	48022A4A2DAE	fe80::4a02:2aff:fe4a:2dae
CN: TP-LINK TECHNOLOGIES CO. LTD.	50C7BF4CF802	50c7bf4cf802
CN: Wistron Infocomm (Zhongshan) Corporation	F80F4142D110	192.168.86.38
CN: Wistron Infocomm (Zhongshan) Corporation	F80F4142D110	f80f4142d110
CN: Wistron Infocomm (Zhongshan) Corporation	F80F4142D110	fe80::6d9a:7ea0:5026:d87e
CN: Zhejiang shenghui lighting co. Ltd	B0CE18189451	192.168.86.28
CN: Zhejiang shenghui lighting co. Ltd	B0CE18189451	b0ce18189451
CN: Zhejiang shenghui lighting co. Ltd	B0CE18189451	fe80::b2ce:18ff:fe18:9451
KR: Samsung Electronics Co. Ltd	900628FB11BB	900628fb11bb
KR: Samsung Electronics Co. Ltd	900628FB11BB	fe80::9206:28ff:fefb:11bb
TW: ASUSTek COMPUTER INC.	0015F25CF374	0015f25cf374
TW: ASUSTek COMPUTER INC.	0015F25CF374	192.168.86.47
TW: ASUSTek COMPUTER INC.	0015F25CF374	fe80::8103:ed8e:c718:82ad
US: Amazon Technologies Inc.	40B4CDB12685	0.0.0.0
US: Amazon Technologies Inc.	40B4CDB12685	192.168.86.27
US: Amazon Technologies Inc.	40B4CDB12685	40b4cdb12685
US: Amazon Technologies Inc.	40B4CDB12685	fe80::42b4:cdff:feb1:2685
US: Amazon Technologies Inc.	747548914299	0.0.0.0
US: Amazon Technologies Inc.	747548914299	192.168.86.39
US: Amazon Technologies Inc.	747548914299	747548914299
US: Amazon Technologies Inc.	747548914299	fe80::7675:48ff:fe91:4299

Figure 5-18. *Excerpt of the manufacturer report*

3. Country report - Much like the manufacturer report, the data is organized by observed country. Included in the report is the number of connections made to systems within the targeted country. Again, during the sensor phase, any country connections not observed during the recording period generate an alert. Figure 5-19 shows an example of the country report.

Country Report 2017-12-30@20:19 UTC

Unique Country Observations

Country	Count
	357228
Canada	29
Czech Republic	1439
Germany	12
Hong Kong	400
Internal	1085886
Ireland	804
Japan	50
Luxembourg	17
Netherlands	832
Singapore	420
Sweden	16
United Kingdom	834
United States	762871

Figure 5-19. *Report observed country connections*

4. Port usage report – This report organizes the data by observed port connections. The report contains each used port number and associated name, along with the unique source and destination IP

addresses, frame type, and associated protocol that was used. Figure 5-20 depicts an excerpt from the port usage report.

Port Usage Report 2017-12-30@20:19 UTC

Port Usage Observations

Port	PortName	Src IP	Dst IP	Frame	Protocol
53	Domain Name Server	192.168.86.1	192.168.86.36	IPV4	UDP
53	Domain Name Server	192.168.86.1	192.168.86.47	IPV4	UDP
53	Domain Name Server	192.168.86.36	192.168.86.1	IPV4	UDP
53	Domain Name Server	192.168.86.47	192.168.86.1	IPV4	UDP
53	Domain Name Server	8.8.8.8	192.168.86.23	IPV4	UDP
53	Domain Name Server	8.8.8.8	192.168.86.25	IPV4	UDP
68	Bootstrap Protocol Client	192.168.86.36	192.168.86.1	IPV4	UDP
68	Bootstrap Protocol Client	192.168.86.37	192.168.86.1	IPV4	UDP
68	Bootstrap Protocol Client	192.168.86.38	192.168.86.1	IPV4	UDP
68	Bootstrap Protocol Client	192.168.86.47	192.168.86.1	IPV4	UDP

Figure 5-20. *Port usage report*

5. Known ICS port usage report and IoT port usage report – These reports further filter the port usage to the only ports that are typically utilized by ICS or IoT devices. It is important to note that some of the port reports can have non-ICS/IoT usage as well. Thus, the reports are named Possible ICS and Possible IoT Port Usage. Report Excerpts E and F provide samples of these reports. During sensor operation, any ICS or IoT observations that did not exist during the recording period will generate an alert. See Figures 5-21 and 5-22 for samples of the ICS and IoT reports.

ICS Report 2017-12-30@20:19 UTC

Possible ICS Observations

Port	Count	Port Name	MAC Address	SRC MFG	DST MFG
443	1	HTTP protocol over TLS/SSL	E4F042BF5185	CN: Wistron Infocomm (Zhongshan) Corporation	Unknown
443	2	HTTP protocol over TLS/SSL	E4F042BF5185	CN: Wistron Infocomm (Zhongshan) Corporation	Unknown
443	8	HTTP protocol over TLS/SSL	E4F042BF5185	CN: Wistron Infocomm (Zhongshan) Corporation	Unknown
443	1	HTTP protocol over TLS/SSL	E4F042BF5185	TW: ASUSTek COMPUTER INC.	Unknown

Figure 5-21. *ICS report sample*

IoT Report 2017-12-30@20:19 UTC

Possible IoT Observations

Observed	Src IP	Dst IP	
84	192.168.86.44	224.0.0.251	
Src Port	**SrcPort Name**	**Dst Port/strong>**	**DstPort Name**
5353	Unknown	5353	Unknown
Src MAC	**Src MFG**	**Dst MAC**	**Dst MFG**
000C8A979D36	US: Bose Corporation	01005E0000FB	
Observed	**Src IP**	**Dst IP**	
58	192.168.86.47	224.0.0.251	
Src Port	**SrcPort Name**	**Dst Port/strong>**	**DstPort Name**
5353	Unknown	5353	Unknown
Src MAC	**Src MFG**	**Dst MAC**	**Dst MFG**
0015F25CF374	TW: ASUSTek COMPUTER INC.	01005E0000FB	
Observed	**Src IP**	**Dst IP**	
106	fe80::8103:ed8e:c718:82ad	ff02::fb	
Src Port	**SrcPort Name**	**Dst Port/strong>**	**DstPort Name**
5353	Unknown	5353	Unknown
Src MAC	**Src MFG**	**Dst MAC**	**Dst MFG**
0015F25CF374	TW: ASUSTek COMPUTER INC.	3333000000FB	

Figure 5-22. *IoT report sample*

Now that we have a recorded baseline, we can use that baseline to activate the sensor by selecting the specific baseline, as shown in Figure 5-23. The report folder is still required, and the activate sensor button will not be available until both report folder and baseline have been selected. The report folder is necessary, as any alerts generated by the sensor will be stored one level below the report folder in a subfolder named ALERTS. It should be noted that all the reports, alerts, and baselines include the ***yyyy-mm-dd-hh-mm*** prefix.

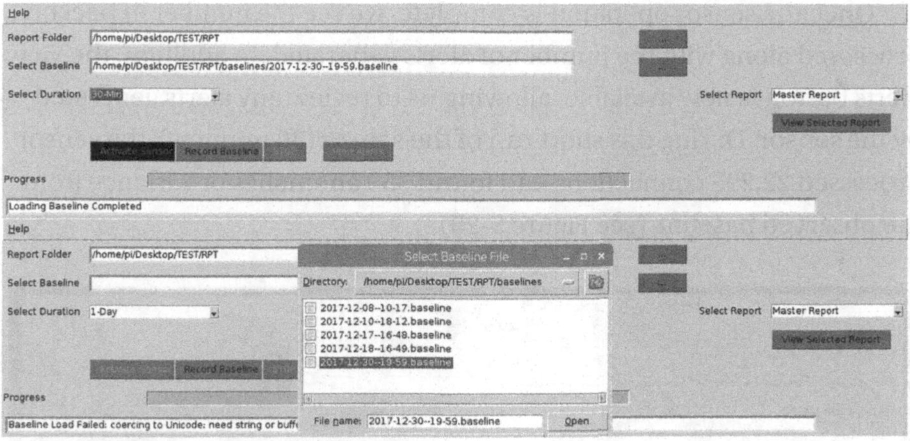

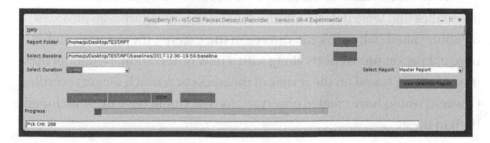

Figure 5-23. *Baseline selection*

Finally, we need to select the duration of the sensor operation and click the activate sensor button; then, the process of monitoring for any variance from the recorded baseline commences (see Figure 5-24).

Figure 5-24. *Activating the sensor*

Once the sensor operation is complete, we see the number of packets processed along with the number of alerts generated. In addition, the view alerts button is now available, allowing us to review any alerts generated by the sensor. During this short run of the sensor (30 minutes), the sensor processed 22,295 connections and found 353 anomalies or variance from the observed baseline (see Figure 5-25).

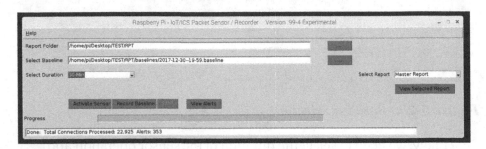

Figure 5-25. *Sensor completed*

We can now examine the generated alerts to view the variance or anomalies that were detected by the sensor. Report Figure 5-26 provides an abbreviated output. As you can see in the excerpt, the report included unusual packet time reports along with a new observation. Neither of these is too serious, based on the review of the packets. A much longer recording (a week) would have created observations that would have likely included both of these.

Alert Report 2017-12-31@16:06 UTC

Alert Observations

Alert	Unusual Packet Time	Alerts-Observed	7
Last Observed	Sun Dec 31 11:03:17 2017		
SrcIP	DstIP	Frame-Type	Protocol
209.133.212.170	192.168.86.21	IPV4	TCP
SrcPort	SrcPortName	DstPort	DstPortName
7024	Unknown	39375	Unknown
SrcMAC	DstMAC	PckSize	
E4F042BF5185	AECA05FA0552	40	
SrcCountry	DstCountry	SrcMFG	DstMFG
United States	Internal	Unknown	Unknown
Alert	Unusual Packet Time	Alerts-Observed	8
Last Observed	Sun Dec 31 11:04:16 2017		
SrcIP	DstIP	Frame-Type	Protocol
192.168.86.33	224.0.0.251	IPV4	IGMP
SrcPort	SrcPortName	DstPort	DstPortName
NA	NA	NA	NA
SrcMAC	DstMAC	PckSize	
B827EBC183AE	01005E0000FB	32	
SrcCountry	DstCountry	SrcMFG	DstMFG
Internal	Unknown	US: Raspberry Pi Foundation	Unknown
Alert	New Observation	Alerts-Observed	1
Last Observed	Sun Dec 31 10:50:14 2017		
SrcIP	DstIP	Frame-Type	Protocol
192.168.86.33	50.116.52.97	IPV4	UDP
SrcPort	SrcPortName	DstPort	DstPortName
123	Network Time Protocol	123	Network Time Protocol
SrcMAC	DstMAC	PckSize	
B827EBC183AE	E4F042BF5185	76	
SrcCountry	DstCountry	SrcMFG	DstMFG
Internal	United States	US: Raspberry Pi Foundation	Unknown

Figure 5-26. *Alert report sample*

Summary

This chapter provided a walk-through of a Raspberry Pi sensor. This
included the following:

- Overview of the sensor connection to an active
  network.

- Recording a baseline.

- Generating and examining reports created during the
  process of recording a baseline.

- Selection of a recorded baseline once created for use during the sensor phase.

- Activation of the sensor based on a specific recorded baseline.

- Examination of alerts generated by the sensor.

In Chapter 6, we will take a detailed look at the recording of the baseline process, and the method of reduction that is accomplished using a Python dictionary. In addition, we will examine the details of the sensor decision-making process and baseline comparison.

CHAPTER 6

Adding Finishing Touches

As with most hardware solutions, they are never finished until they are no longer relevant. This chapter adds a couple of final touches to this version of the Pi sensor. As this book proceeds to print, I'm sure more changes, updates, and enhancements will continue. Not to worry, the updates and source code for the latest changes will be available via git-hub. Go to www.apress.com/9781484236994.

Raspberry Pi Latest Version

On Pi Day 2018 (March 14, i.e., 3.14), the Raspberry Pi foundation announced the release of the Raspberry Pi 3 Model B+. According to the foundation, the new improvements allow the computer to sustain higher performance for longer periods of time (see Figure 6-1).

© Chet Hosmer 2018
C. Hosmer, *Defending IoT Infrastructures with the Raspberry Pi*,
https://doi.org/10.1007/978-1-4842-3700-7_6

Figure 6-1. *Raspberry Pi 3 Model B+*

The 3B+ upgrade offers a faster processor (200MHz increase in CPU clock frequency), better thermal management, three times the wired and wireless network throughput, and Gigabit Ethernet. These improvements add value to our sensor solution by delivering additional speed to process packets faster without overheating the Pi.

Adding a new rugged case with a built-in fan (see Figure 6-2) adds greater stability, sleekness, and cooling to the sensor.

Figure 6-2. *Raspberry Pi in ruggedized Smraza case*

As of this writing, the multilayer Smraza case is available from Amazon, among other places. The case includes an on/off switch cable, a fan, and heat sinks.

Sensor Software Updates

Along with the new Raspberry Pi 3 Model B+, several important software updates were made to the sensor. They include NIC selection and MAC address filtering, as shown in Figure 6-3 and labeled A and B respectively.

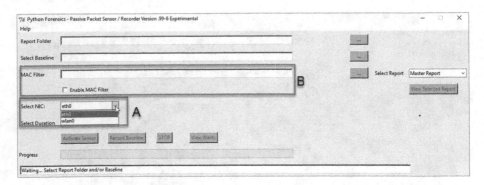

Figure 6-3. *Sensor updates: (A) NIC selection; (B) MAC address filtering*

(A) NIC Selection

Determining the available interfaces on the Raspberry Pi is quite straightforward. The directory /sys/class/net holds the names of the available interfaces. For our purposes, this allows us to provide a drop-down list of possible interfaces and most importantly allows the selection of the wireless interface in addition to the standard Ethernet port. As mentioned in the preceding, both interfaces have been significantly improved on the Raspberry Pi 3 Model B+.

To build a list and the GUI drop-down menu, see Listing 6-1.

Listing 6-1. Targeting Specific Devices to Monitor

```
try:
    nicList = os.listdir('/sys/class/net')
    nicList.sort()
    nicTuple = tuple(nicList)
except:
    nicTuple= tuple(['eth0'])

self.ethPort['values'] = nicTuple
self.ethPort.current(0)
self.ethPort.grid(row=5, column=1, padx=5, pady=10, sticky='w')
```

Note, for example, if you select the wireless LAN (wlan0), you must first connect to the desired wireless network to monitor. On the Raspberry Pi you can select, connect, and log in to the desired wireless interface using the icon in the upper right corner (see Figure 6-4).

Figure 6-4. *Raspberry Pi wireless selection*

(B) MAC Address Filtering

The second addition included in finishing touches is the ability to monitor, record, and activate the sensor to target specific MAC addresses. Within industrial control or compartmentalized IoT environments, it is quite common to closely monitor critical assets. This selection uses a list of MAC addresses supplied in a flat text file. Figures 6-5 and 6-6 demonstrate the selection of the MAC filter file and the check box that enables MAC filtering.

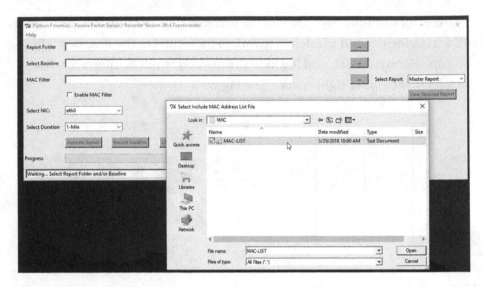

Figure 6-5. *Selection of the MAC filtering list*

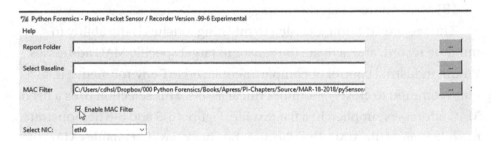

Figure 6-6. *Enabling the MAC filter*

The MAC-LIST text file contains a simple list of MAC addresses, one per line, as shown in Figure 6-7.

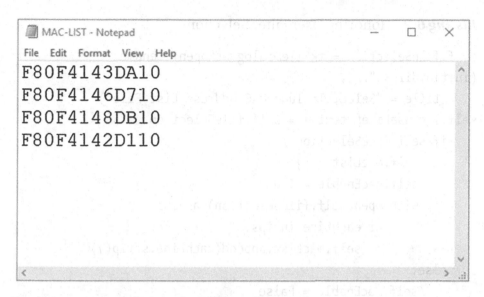

Figure 6-7. Sample MAC-LIST text file

You might be questioning why we chose to use a MAC address for filtering instead of the IP address. IP addresses for devices are dynamically assigned by DHCP unless they are statically defined. Therefore, using MAC addresses (which can be manipulated as well, but require targeted action to do so) provides better filtering options. When the sensor is operated, only packets with source or destination MAC addresses provided in the list will be recorded. This allows for easier analysis of the reports such as port usage and country, allowing you to verify the inbound and outbound traffic from specific devices.

The MAC address filtering is handled in just a few lines of code. First, we create a list of MACs to filter when a MAC filtering file is provided, and MAC filtering is enabled (see Listing 6-2).

Listing 6-2. Honoring User Filter Selections

```
self.fileSelection = tkFileDialog.askopenfilename
(initialdir = "./",
    title = "Select Include MAC Address List File")
self.IncludeFile['text'] = self.fileSelection
   if self.fileSelection:
       self.macList = []
       self.macEnable = True
       with open(self.fileSelection) as ips:
           for eachLine in ips:
               self.macList.append(eachLine.strip())
   else:
       self.macEnable = False
```

This method provides easy filtering of MAC addresses during packet extraction (see Listing 6-3).

Listing 6-3. Filtering Out Other Device Packets

```
ethernetHeader=packet[0:ETH_LEN]
ethFields =struct.unpack("!6s6sH",ethernetHeader)

# Extract DST MAC, SRC MAC and Frame Type
self.dstMac = hexlify(ethFields[0]).upper()
self.srcMac = hexlify(ethFields[1]).upper()

# Check if MAC Filtering is on
if self.macFilterEnable and self.macFilterSet:
    if not (self.dstMac in self.macFilter) and
        not (self.srcMac in self.macFilter):
        # Filter this packet
        return
```

Summary

This chapter added some finishing touches to the Raspberry Pi sensor, specifically, the ability to monitor any network interface that is available on the Pi. This provides a wider view of activity on the network in question.

In addition, the capability to target specific MAC addresses detected during recording or sensor activation further refines the applications of the Pi sensor.

In Chapter 7, we will discuss future capabilities that are planned for the Pi sensor, and how you can participate in the project.

CHAPTER 7

Future Work

Continued advancement of the Pi sensor is actively underway. Key areas of development include the following:

1. Expansion of key lookup tables

2. Implementation of user searching and filtering of scan results

3. Headless communication with remotely deployed Pi sensors

4. Correlation of results from a swarm of Pi sensors

Expansion of Lookup Tables

The Pi Sensor utilizes several key lookup tables that have been compiled for open source websites. They include port, manufacturer, and country lookups.

Port Lookups

The port lookup table is gathered from the IANA at `www.iana.org`. IANA provides registration services for port numbers designed for a specific purpose. However, many of the port usage descriptions provide only general information regarding port usage. Additional details are necessary

© Chet Hosmer 2018
C. Hosmer, *Defending IoT Infrastructures with the Raspberry Pi*,
https://doi.org/10.1007/978-1-4842-3700-7_7

to better map port usage to specific IoT and ICS applications. This would allow for more accurate reporting, tracking, and usage of ports by IoT and ICS applications.

Manufacturer Lookup

Looking up manufactures by the OUI suffers from some of the same limitations of the port lookup. The OUI represents the first 24 bits of the MAC address emitted by devices. The OUI is managed by the IEEE. The specific OUI values are purchased from the IEEE and added to the registry. The issue is that the OUI represents the manufacturer but does not define the use or application of the value. For example, identification of which OUI numbers are associated with drones, entertainment devices, computers, home automation, industrial control, cybersecurity devices, and so on is not readily available. If more details and cross-referencing of OUI and a specific category were available, then the ability to track behaviors of IoT devices would be significantly improved. This categorization coupled with a more refined port usage would allow the detection of normal and aberrant communication between IoT devices and between IoT devices and local/remote communicating/controlling entities.

Country Lookup

The expansion, accuracy, and refinement of country lookup would help to identify potential hostile or inappropriate communications between devices. IP addresses are managed by IANA along with five regional Internet registries. Tracking and associating IP addresses to a finer-grained location (i.e., street address or lat/lon location) would provide more detailed location information of potential attackers, botnets, and command and control servers.

Implementation of User Searches and Filtering of Scan Result

One of the immediate next steps to PiSensor is the development of an interface that would allow mining of scan and alert results. This feature needs to engage the user in actively reviewing the results of recording and/or alert results. This interface needs to be interactive and would help pinpoint activities of interest. This information would be used for early indication and warning, alert refinement and digital forensics, incident response (DFIR) activities.

Headless Communication with Remotely Deployed Pi Sensors

The current GUI for direct interaction with the Pi sensor provides a good local method of configuration, activation, control, and review of Pi sensor results. However, the ability to place Pi sensors in remote locations and then control and retrieve results and alerts is the logical next step. This would allow the deployment in either wired or wireless settings with only a power source and connection to the network to be monitored. This would eliminate the need for a monitor, keyboard, and mouse, and would reduce the cost of deployment to under $50.00 per sensor. This would of course require the Pi sensor to support a secure interface with those controlling its operation. Examining possible security devices for this purpose (note that software-only devices have been discounted due to the potential security risks), I have begun to experiment with the ZYMKEY 4i, shown in Figures 7-1 and 7-2.

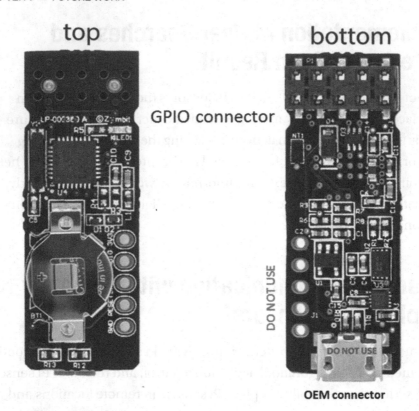

Figure 7-1. *ZYMKEY from zymbit*

Figure 7-2. *ZYMKEY install on a Raspberry Pi*

The ZYMKEY provides a hardware key that connects to the Raspberry Pi I2C bus. The ZYMKEY comes with a Python application interface allowing us to integrate the key into the Pi sensor application. The device includes a cryptographic processing and authentication engine, a secure key store, and tamper detection and response circuits. In addition, when placed in production mode the ZYMKEY binds itself to the specific Raspberry Pi it is connected to and will not operate on a different Pi. This combined with the tamper detection and response and secure key store allows us to perform secure authentication and encryption with a control center.

The general operating concept is to develop a secure console that can activate, control, and receive alerts from remotely deployed Pi sensors as shown in Figure 7-3.

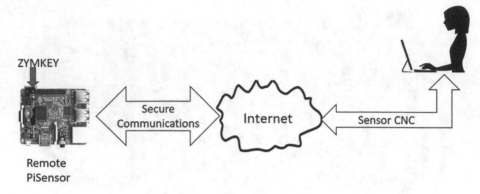

Figure 7-3. *Secure command and control of a remote Pi sensor*

Correlation of Results from a Swarm of Pi Sensors

The concept of swarm deployment of sensors is certainly not new. However, doing so with a group of Raspberry Pi's acting as a swarm of IoT devices is. This final area of future work is still being researched at this point.

The need for this is straightforward. Organizations now need to deploy sensors at numerous locations within a single facility, facilities across town, or across the world, and this need will continue to grow. Consider a hotel with thousands of rooms and hundreds of floors. The ability to detect behaviors and instrument the Pi sensor with various wireless and physical sensing capabilities would provide early indications of nefarious activities or even aid hotel guests in distress. My building a swarm or Pi's provides not only discrete communication from Pi to a command and control center, but also Pi-to-Pi sharing of information.

Raspberry Pi Sensor: Executing the Sensor on Your Raspberry Pi

The easiest method is to simply download the prebuilt executable for the Pi sensor. The executable is delivered as a Debian package. Download the package file piSensor.deb and then install it.

```
sudo dpkg -i piSensor.deb
```

The second method is to download the source code and execute the PiSensor directly from the Python source: follow the README instructions in the source download.

The piSensor.deb and piSensor.zip are both available as part of the source code for this book. Go to www.apress.com/us/book/9781484236994 and click the source code button.

Summary

This chapter provided a look at the next steps for the PiSensor. If you would like to contribute ideas, write some code, or test future work, please contact the author directly.

Coming up next is the appendix. The appendix provides the complete source code for PiSensor along with samples of hotlist and MAC-LIST text files.

APPENDIX A

Obtaining the Python Source Code

As noted in the Chapter 7 summary, the source code is continually evolving, and new versions are continually updated. As my wife Janet (also an outstanding computer scientist) remarks, "software is never done until it is obsolete."

Obtaining the Source Code

Readers can obtain a copy of the current Python source code, additional files, and an executable version for the Raspberry Pi on GitHub via the book's product page, located at

www.apress.com/978-1-4842-3699-4

In addition, for those wishing to participate in the advancement of the code for the Raspberry Pi or porting the code to other platforms, please contact the author:

Chet Hosmer, cdh@python-forensics.org

or

visit the web page www.python-forensics.org.

© Chet Hosmer 2018
C. Hosmer, *Defending IoT Infrastructures with the Raspberry Pi*,
https://doi.org/10.1007/978-1-4842-3700-7

Source Code Copyright and Licensing

The following copyright message is included in each of the source files for the Raspberry Pi sensor/recorder to clearly state the use and distribution of the source code.

'''

```
Packet Sensor/Recorder GUI Version
Version 1.0 May 5, 2018 Cinco-de-Mayo Version

Copyright (c) 2018 Python Forensics and Chet Hosmer

Permission is hereby granted, free of charge, to any person
obtaining a copy of this software and associated documentation
files (the "Software"), to deal in the Software without
restriction, including without limitation the rights to use, copy,
modify, merge, publish, distribute, sublicense, and/or sell copies
of the Software, and to permit persons to whom the software is
furnished to do so, subject to the following condition:

The above copyright notice and this permission notice shall be
included in all copies or substantial portions of the Software.
```

'''

Glossary

Active Discovery – The act of directly probing devices attached to a network to discover them along with the services they have open and even to determine the type of operating system or device (e.g., Windows, Linux, Mac, Printer).

Arduino – An open source electronics platform based on available and simple-to-use hardware and software components.

ARP – Address Resolution Protocol. This protocol is used to map IP addresses to a unique physical MAC address.

HTTP – Hypertext Transfer Protocol. An application-layer protocol for communicating using hypermedia.

ICMP – Internet Control Message Protocol. ICMPv4 is used for IPv4 environments, and ICMPv6 is used for IPv6 environments. The protocol is used to identify and troubleshoot network and host connection issues. It should be noted that in many modern environments ICMP packets are blocked.

IGMP – Protocol used to establish multicast group memberships.

IIoT – Industrial Internet of Things. It should be noted that this acronym is frowned upon in many circles, because the "I" in "IoT" stands for Internet, and most industrial users would never attach their control systems to the Internet.

IoT – Internet of Things.

IP – Internet Protocol. Utilized by networked devices to connect and communicate.

JMS – Java Message Service. Developed by Sun Microsystems to provide a standard method for Java programs to communicate using asynchronous messaging at the enterprise level.

© Chet Hosmer 2018
C. Hosmer, *Defending IoT Infrastructures with the Raspberry Pi*,
https://doi.org/10.1007/978-1-4842-3700-7

MAC – Media Access Control address of a network interface. Computers and other network devices may have one or more network interfaces, and each would have a unique MAC address. The MAC address is defined by the manufacturer of devices.

NETBIOS – Network Basic Input/Output System. NETBIOS is an application interface and not a networking protocol.

NIC – Network Interface Card.

OUI – Organizationally Unique Identifier. The first 24 bits of the device MAC address (in most cases) represents the manufacturer of the device. These are purchased from the IEEE (Institute of Electrical and Electronics Engineers).

Passive Monitoring – The act of monitoring (sniffing) network traffic to record behaviors over a period. The concept allows for a deeper look at the activities of network devices even when those devices might be transient or devices that may not respond to normal probing.

PaPirus Display –An ePaper display technology that mimics the appearance of ink on paper. ePaper displays reflected light, much like ordinary paper. These displays are capable of holding text and images indefinitely, even in the absence of power.

Pickle – A Python Standard Library that allows serialization of Python objects (e.g., strings, lists, sets, dictionaries). The serialization allows for the fast storage and retrieval of these objects.

Python – A general-purpose, open source, high-level programming language.

Raspberry Pi – A credit card–sized (and smaller) single-board computer developed in the United Kingdom by the Raspberry Pi Foundation.

Raspbian – One of the many flavors of operating systems available for the Raspberry Pi.

SMB –Server Message Block. A communication protocol that allows for the sharing of files, printers, and other I/O devices between computers.

SOAP – Simple Object Access Protocol. Provides messaging services allowing programs that execute on different operating systems to communicate using HTTP and XML.

SPAN Port – Sometimes referred to as a monitoring port available on modern switches and routers. All traffic that passes through the switch or router can also be directed to this port. This allows monitoring devices to observe all traffic flowing the switch.

SQL – Structured Query Language. A standard language used for interfacing with relational databases.

TCP – Transaction Control Protocol. It operates at the transport layer, as its primary role is to establish and maintain connections between host computers and devices.

Tcl/Tk – A scripting language developed by Sun Microsystems for creating graphical user interfaces.

TKinter – Python library that provides an object-oriented layer on top of Tcl/Tk to provide graphical user interface capabilities to Python.

TLS – Transport Layer Security. As the name implies, it ensures privacy and tamper protection between server and client or even between peer-to-peer entities.

UDP – User Datagram Protocol. The protocol does not verify receipt of transmitted packets and requires no response. Therefore, the protocol is referred to as an unreliable link protocol, whereas TCP is commonly referred to as a reliable link protocol. Both operate at the transport layer.

uPnP – Universal Plug and Play. A networking protocol that allows devices such as IoT, computers, phones, printers, and so on to discover their presences on a network.

WeMo – A series of products, developed by Belkin International, that enable users to access, monitor, and control devices over the Internet from anywhere.

XML –eXtensible Markup Language. Defines encoding rules for documents that can be utilized across the Internet.

Zero Configuration – Many IoT devices can configure themselves and join a network without manual intervention. All configuration of these devices is done automatically simply by applying power. This generates a network ready state, allowing the device to discover and be discovered.

Z-Wave – A wireless communication protocol typically used for home IoT devices such as lighting, entertainment, and appliances.

ZigBee – A specification for a communication protocol used in personal area networks typically built from small, low-power devices. ZigBee is based on the 802.15.4 specification.

Index

A

Address Resolution Protocol (ARP)
    packets, 23–24

B, C

Baseline
    activating sensor, 147
    alert report sample, 148
    IoT report sample, 145
    manufacturer report
        excerpt, 142
    master report excerpt, 140–141
    PaPirus recording progress
        display, 138–139
    port usage report, 144
    recording progress, 137
    report folder and duration, 137
    report folder selection, 136
    report selection, 139
    selection, 146

D

Device-to-cloud communications, 4
Device-to-device
    communication, 3–4

Device-to-gateway framework, 5
Dynamic Discovery
    Protocols, 10

E, F, G

Ethernet packet, 21–22

H

Headless communication, remote
    Pi sensor, 163–166

I, J, K

Internet Control Message Protocol
    (ICMP) packets, 27
Internet Protocol (IP)
    packets, 24
IoT Security Compliance
    Framework, 6
IoT vulnerabilities
    attack vectors, 11
    compliance classification
        security objectives, 7
    deployment options, 3
    devices, autonomous/
        semiautonomous, 1

© Chet Hosmer 2018
C. Hosmer, *Defending IoT Infrastructures with the Raspberry Pi*,
https://doi.org/10.1007/978-1-4842-3700-7

Printed in the United States
By Bookmasters